The Ge
Teacher's Handbook

Continuum Education Handbooks

A companion website to accompany this book is available online at:

http://education.best.continuumbooks.com

Please visit the link and register with us to receive your password and access these downloadable resources.

If you experience any problems accessing the resources, please contact Continuum at: info@continuumbooks.com

Also available in the Continuum Education Handbooks Series

The History Teacher's Handbook, Neil Smith
The Art and Design Teacher's Handbook, Susie Hodge
The Citizenship Teacher's Handbook, Kate Brown and Stephen Fairbrass

Also available from Continuum

100 Ideas for Teaching Geography, Andy Leeder

The Geography Teacher's Handbook

Brin Best

continuum

Continuum International Publishing Group
The Tower Building
11 York Road
London SE1 7NX

80 Maiden Lane
Suite 704
New York NY 10038

www.continuumbooks.com

British Library Cataloguing-in-Publication Data
A catalogue record for this book is available from the British Library.

ISBN: 978-1-8470-6167-6 (paperback)

Library of Congress Cataloging-in-Publication Data
Best, Brin.
The geography teacher's handbook / Brin Best.
p. cm. – (Continuum education handbooks)
ISBN 978-1-84706-167-6 – ISBN 978-1-4411-4620-5 – ISBN 978-1-4411-5479-8 1. Geography–Study and teaching (Secondary) I. Title. II. Series.

G73.B515 2011
910.71′2–dc22

2010052884

Typeset by Newgen Imaging Systems Pvt Ltd, Chennai, India
Printed and bound in India

Contents

Acknowledgements

I am especially grateful to my former colleagues in the geography department at Settle High School and Community College, with whom I worked for eight years. In particular I want to place on record the key role of Bob Hordern as a role model and mentor for outstanding geography teaching. I am also grateful to all the students I taught and from whom I learned so much about what does and doesn't work in the classroom. I particularly want to thank them for their willingness to engage in the creative, unusual and sometimes downright balmy lessons that I prepared for them. I enjoyed every day that I was lucky enough to teach them.

As well as contributing the case studies, Sophie Craven read through the entire manuscript and made many comments that helped to improve the final version. I am also grateful to Alan Kinder and Alan Parkinson for their support of the project. Finally, I want to thank my wife, Amanda, and parents for unfailing support during the preparation of this book.

A note about key stages and year groups

Throughout the book, reference is made to key stages and year groups which are specific to the education system in England and Wales. The following key explains what these terms mean.

Year 7: 11 to 12 years old
Year 8: 12 to 13 years old
Year 9: 13 to 14 years old
Year 10: 14 to 15 years old
Year 11: 15 to 16 years old
Year 12: 16 to 17 years old
Year 13: 17 to 18 years old

Key stage 3: 11 to 14 years old
Key stage 4: 14 to 16 years old
Key stage 5: 16 to 18 years old

Key

? This symbol in the margin denotes reflective questions for you to think about

This symbol appears where there is supplementary material or a downloadable version of the text on the companion website

1 Introducing geography

Overview

This chapter provides the background and context for the book. It justifies the place of geography in the twenty-first century and argues that good geographers can be seen as survivors. The chapter invites you to explore your personal vision for geography and goes on to consider the cross-curricular and extra-curricular links and the creative nature of geography teaching. It also discusses the pressures on geography as a subject and asks you to join the mission to reinstate it as a highly relevant and integral part of any modern secondary school syllabus.

Good geographers are *survivors*. There is no doubt that our distant ancestors simply *had* to have supreme geographical knowledge and skills to survive the rigours of their lives. They needed them so they could find things to eat and drink, and then safely navigate their way back to their simple dwellings. They needed them so they knew which hazards they must avoid along their routes, and so they could read the language of the clouds. They eventually needed them so they could ensure their crops would grow to sustain their families. In short, our ancestors were survivors because they valued geographical knowledge and skills.

A lot has changed in the intervening years. We will very soon become a predominantly urban species – with more people on our planet living in built-up areas than in the countryside. Although for many people, navigating their way to the supermarket has replaced the skills to find wild food, humanity is facing other – equally serious – challenges.

- Our planet is heating up, seemingly because of our actions, with potentially very damaging consequences.
- Pollution of our environment is changing ecosystems forever.
- Increasing leisure time in many parts of the world is bringing its own unforeseen problems.
- Urban planners have yet to find the solution to harmonious city life for people of all social groups.
- Despite the easy availability of food and other basic resources in many parts of the world, there are millions of people still living below the poverty line.

For these reasons, and many others like them, we still need good geographers. In fact, I'm convinced that *every* citizen needs to have a good grasp of geography in all its forms. And those who will become our leaders need the best grasp of all.

This book is about how you can inspire, nurture and motivate the next generation of decision-makers through your work as a geography teacher. Remember: the current generation will go on to shape the future of our world.

Your own vision for geography

What's your own personal *vision* for geography? Perhaps this isn't a question you've given much thought to before, but before we get into the nuts and bolts of geographical education, it's a vital question to ask yourself. Why? Because it underpins everything you do as a geography teacher and will serve as a key point of reference now and in the future.

Your vision for geography should encompass some big-picture issues about its place in the world and in our schools. It should address some deep philosophical issues as well as deal with practical day-to-day matters. It should make clear why you became a geography teacher and what core mission guides your work on a day-to-day basis. My belief is that very few geography teachers came into the role by accident: instead, they share a distinctive world view that is different from, say, English or maths teachers. Pause now to reflect on your vision as a geography teacher by answering the following questions:

- Why did you choose the career of geography teaching?
- Why is geography still so important to you today?
- What geographical knowledge, skills, values and attitudes do you want your students to leave school with?
- What kind of preferred future are you working towards, for our world and for your school?
- How, through your day-to-day work as a teacher, will you try to achieve these goals?

A vision should be inspirational and motivating for the person who has created it. Why not write the answers to these questions somewhere special so you can refer to them when the going gets tough? Remember to not be afraid of thinking *big* with your vision. A famous thinker once said: 'Your vision isn't big enough unless people are falling over laughing when they hear about it!'

Cross-curricular links

Geography teaching in our schools takes place within the context of a host of other subjects and disciplines. As teachers, it is our role to make geography distinctive while also ensuring there is a good 'fit' with other areas of the formal and informal curriculum. One of the reasons that most students find geography innately interesting and useful is because it has immediate relevance to their lives. It also has a key contribution to make in creating rounded individuals.

For example, geography can help to develop problem-solving and decision-making skills which are essential for a happy and productive life – as well as helping young people to pass their exams.

Throughout this book, links will be made to the ways in which geography can form part of the wider web of learning taking place in your school – and indeed beyond it. Reflect now for a few moments on what that web looks like in your context:

?

- How well is geography integrated into the whole curriculum in your school?
- How are students shown how to transfer the skills they have learned in the geography classroom?
- What contribution does geography make to other aspects of your school, such as citizenship education, the global dimension and the development of functional skills?

You will have the chance to do some more thinking about these issues later in the book, through some targeted tasks. They will help you to see that whenever you teach a geography lesson, for every one of students your teaching forms just one part of a much wider web of learning.

Creativity for geography

I happen to believe that geography teachers have always tended to be among the most *creative* teachers in a school. I think it's partly due to the nature of the subject and the kinds of learning that are possible when you teach geography. But I'm sure it's also due to the creative spirit of most geography teachers, inspired as they are by wilderness, the natural world, the intriguing geography of settlements or whatever else makes them tick. Geography also allows us to get outside into the wider world – or as I often like to see it, the *real world* – with young people, so we can let their spirits free, too. Here, the wind can mess up their hair, they can get soaked to the skin and they can be inspired by what exists outside their predominantly centrally heated world. Geography really does provide a rich playground for creativity.

Throughout my own career as a geography teacher and subject leader, I tried to model a highly creative approach to teaching. I knew I had made an important step forward when four years into my first teaching job, a group of year 10 General Certificate of

Secondary Education (GCSE) students chose to present the impact of Hurricane Andrew through the medium of an elaborate puppet show – and I wasn't fazed by the prospect! I'm glad I let them do it, as I'm glad I let that rather far-fetched costumed role play on the rainforest to take place, and that brilliant decision-making exercise on the local wind farm that we filmed for prosperity. Some of the participating students – now with their own children – still talk about those lessons. These experiences have convinced me that to truly bring geography alive, we need to revel in the creative possibilities of the subject and help all the young people we work with to develop their own creative skills. This is a central message running through this book.

The pressures on geography

I'm sure you've got the message by now that I'm tirelessly optimistic about what geography can do – how it can open minds and open doors to a whole new world of discovery. But I'm also aware that geography as a subject is under pressure in our schools. In fact, I'd go further than that: I think it is in danger of being squeezed into insignificance.

There are many reasons for this. One of them is the huge wealth of choice now given to students in schools. I used to have five GCSE teaching groups in my department, whereas now many of these students instead choose subjects like business, media studies or IT. These are the kind of pressures affecting all subjects to some extent, but I fear that geography is witnessing a more insidious and damaging phenomenon – it is being marginalized because fewer and fewer people feel it offers something *distinctive* and *valuable* to the curriculum at school. While the views of such people must be challenged and are surely based on misconceptions, there is no denying their effect, with fewer and fewer students taking geography and universities seeing an associated decline in geography undergraduates.

The UK National Action Plan for Geography, which launched in 2006, was initiated to address some of these issues, but there is still much work to do. If you accept my analysis, then it is surely up to all of us who are passionate about geography to join a mission to reinstate the subject as an essential part of any twenty-first-century curriculum. My hope is that by presenting a wealth of exciting and innovative teaching and learning strategies for geography in this book, coupled with a simple but rigorous framework underpinning creative geography teaching, I can feed the minds of those at the forefront of the challenge that awaits us. Surely it will be geography teachers who will be on the front line as we try to recover the ground that we have lost. Are you ready to join the mission?

2 Geographical learning models

Overview

This chapter sets out the main models that underpin the rest of the book. It leads the reader through an academically rigorous but highly practical four-stage approach to outstanding geography lessons, which is developed from a tried and tested generic model for effective teaching and learning. This chapter also considers what the essential features are of effective geography lessons. Also introduced is the concept of the creativity cycle, an eight-step approach to developing creativity in the classroom. Do take the time to digest the main messages of this chapter – the rest of the book is written with the assumption that you have a good grasp of these essential models.

There have been many attempts to characterize the essential elements in episodes of teaching and learning. In our book *The Creative Teaching & Learning Toolkit,* Will Thomas and I proposed a new way to think about the key factors to be considered when making judgements about teaching and learning in the form of our *Five Domains of Effective Teaching* (see Figure 2.1). This model has been very well received by teachers and has provided a simple but powerful tool to enable more incisive thinking about really effective teaching and learning.

For the purposes of this book, however, we need to focus in detail on how this model can be used to help design more effective learning experiences in **geography**. In order to do this, I

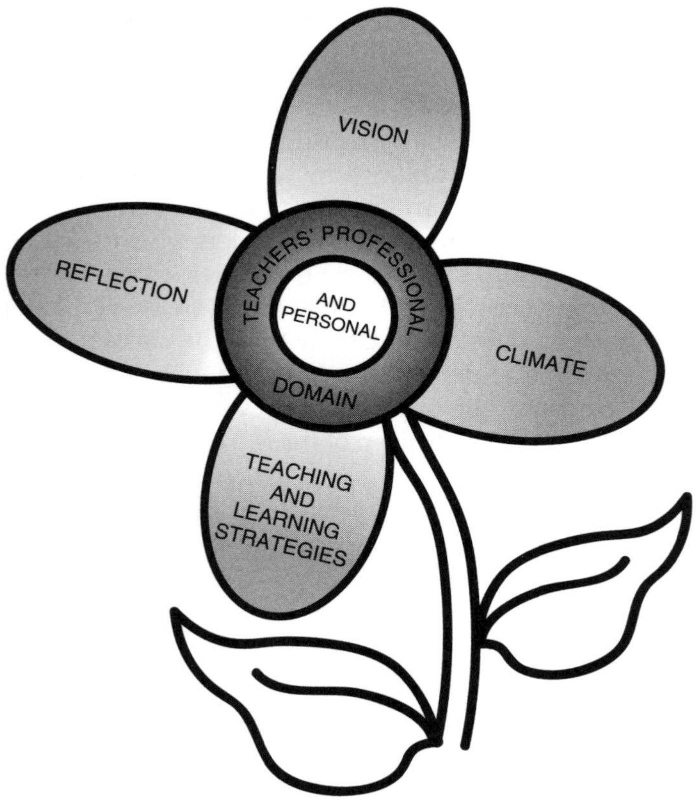

Figure 2.1 The five domains of effective teaching

First published in Best, B., and W. Thomas (2007), *The Creative Teaching & Learning Toolkit*. London: Continuum International Publishing.

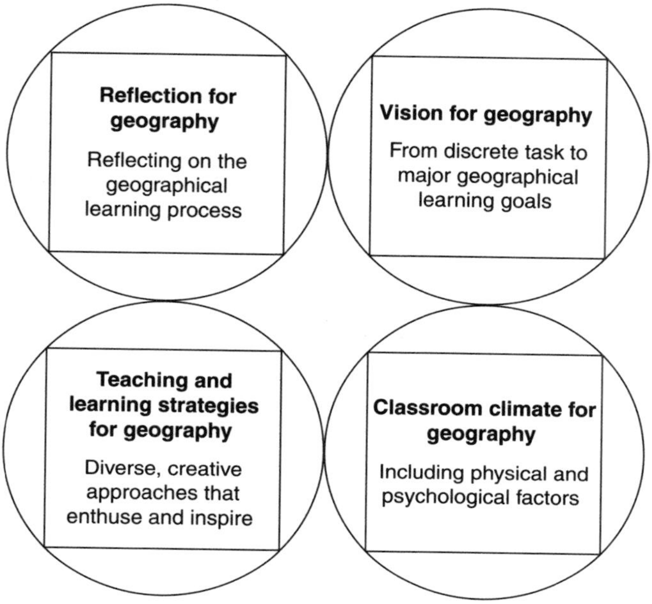

Figure 2.2 The four hemispheres of effective geography teaching

have created a new model which I have called *The Four Hemispheres of Effective Geography Teaching*, as shown in Figure 2.2. The original component of the teacher's personal and professional domain – while highly relevant to the teaching of geography – is beyond the immediate scope of this book, which is concerned with designing engaging and stimulating geography lessons.

The Four Hemispheres of Effective Geography Teaching shows how teachers can focus on four key elements in lesson planning and 'delivery' – vision, climate for learning, teaching and learning strategies, and reflection. I will now consider each of these hemispheres in detail, making practical suggestions in each case for what this means for your classroom.

Vision for geography

Whenever you start planning your teaching – whether it be a complete scheme of work or a discrete activity within a lesson – you should have a clear idea of what you are aiming to achieve. Your *intended outcomes* form the core part of your day-to-day vision for the kind of geographical knowledge and skills you want your students to

Task 2.1: Clarify your vision for geography

Complete the table to help articulate aspects of your vision for geography at a variety of scales. Note that in each case the vision refers to your *intended outcomes* at a range of scales. Record in the 'explanation' column examples that illustrate your vision at each level: for example, the aims of a particular lesson activity or the major goals underpinning your work as a geography teacher. As you work through each, note any actions that suggest themselves.

Scale	Explanation	Suggested new actions
Lesson activity		
Complete lesson		
Unit of work		
Scheme of work		
Major goals for geography teaching		

develop. There is a bigger picture to your vision, too, which concerns your 'major goals' for geography teaching. These are the key concepts, ideas, facts, skills, and values and attitudes that you want to inform – part of everything you do as a teacher. This overarching vision may have a particular emphasis depending on your background or the specifics of your own geographical education or previous jobs (e.g. environmental concerns, urban geography issues, the specifics of physical geography). Task 2.1 will help you to clarify your vision for geography at a range of scales.

Classroom climate for geography

Outstanding geography lessons usually take place when there is a distinctive and effective *classroom climate*. This refers to both the physical (e.g. the use of displays) and psychological aspects (e.g. how you support the emotional needs of students) of your classroom. An effective classroom climate for geography will facilitate every other aspect of your work and the learning of your students. On the other hand, a classroom climate that is not appropriate can hinder learning and can render even innovative teaching

Psychological factors	Physical factors
-Student contentment	-Temperature
-Stress levels	-Oxygen levels
-Emotional support provided	-Stimulating geographical displays for all the senses

Figure 2.3: Classroom climate for geography

and learning approaches ineffective. For this reason, it's vital to think carefully about your own classroom climate and to take practical steps to engineer precisely the kind of climate that is desirable. It's vital to remember that the classroom climate will not simply 'look after itself' if you design fun learning experiences; instead it needs to be planned for. There are key links here with the accelerated learning approach, which is explored further on page 33. Figure 2.3 explores key aspects of classroom climate for geography, and Task 2.2. encourages you to consider in detail your own classroom climate.

Task 2.2: Explore your classroom climate for geography

Study Figure 2.3 and imagine what two or three students in one of your teaching groups might say about the classroom climate you have created. Write down their responses under the headings: physical and psychological. You may later wish to actually do this with some students, perhaps as part of a student 'focus group' activity. What aspects of your classroom climate do you feel you may need to work on? How could you do this? Who else in your school or local authority might support you as you do this? This would be an excellent exercise to carry out in conjunction with another person in your department. You may also wish to consider whether there are any aspects of the classroom climate that seem beyond your immediate control, and what the barriers are to influencing them. Will some whole school measures be needed to help create a better climate for learning in every classroom?

In many schools, the physical factors affecting the climate for learning in classrooms are often neglected. Indeed, some teachers might argue that some of these factors are beyond their immediate control. Task 2.2 invites you to consider this dilemma in further detail.

Teaching and learning for geography

I'm convinced that it is possible to make geography lessons some of the very best learning experiences that students ever witness during their time in school. By this, I mean it is possible to make geographical learning exciting, engaging, challenging, relevant, innovative and fun – all at the same time! I'm convinced of this because I've had the pleasure to work with young people who have told me about geography lessons that they still remember, even though school is otherwise a distant memory. The specific teaching and learning strategies that teachers use to switch young minds on to geography are the key to unlocking the world of outstanding geography lessons. They are your bread and butter as a geography teacher, and if you neglect them, both you and your students will be malnourished intellectually.

There are literally thousands of different teaching and learning strategies that you can use as a geography teacher. Figure 2.4 gives a brief outline of some of the main types, and Task 2.3 asks you to use this diagram to carry out an audit of your preferred teaching and learning approaches.

Analysis of teaching styles in schools has shown that teachers tend to have a predominant style which they habitually use to the exclusion of other styles. This *preferred teaching style* of teachers also encompasses a discrete set of teaching and learning strategies which their students become familiar with. There is a real danger, however, that this preferred teaching style is excluding some students with specific learning preferences which are in contradiction of the teaching style. For this reason, it is really important to vary your teaching style, and the specific teaching and learning approaches that accompany it, to appeal to the widest possible range of students.

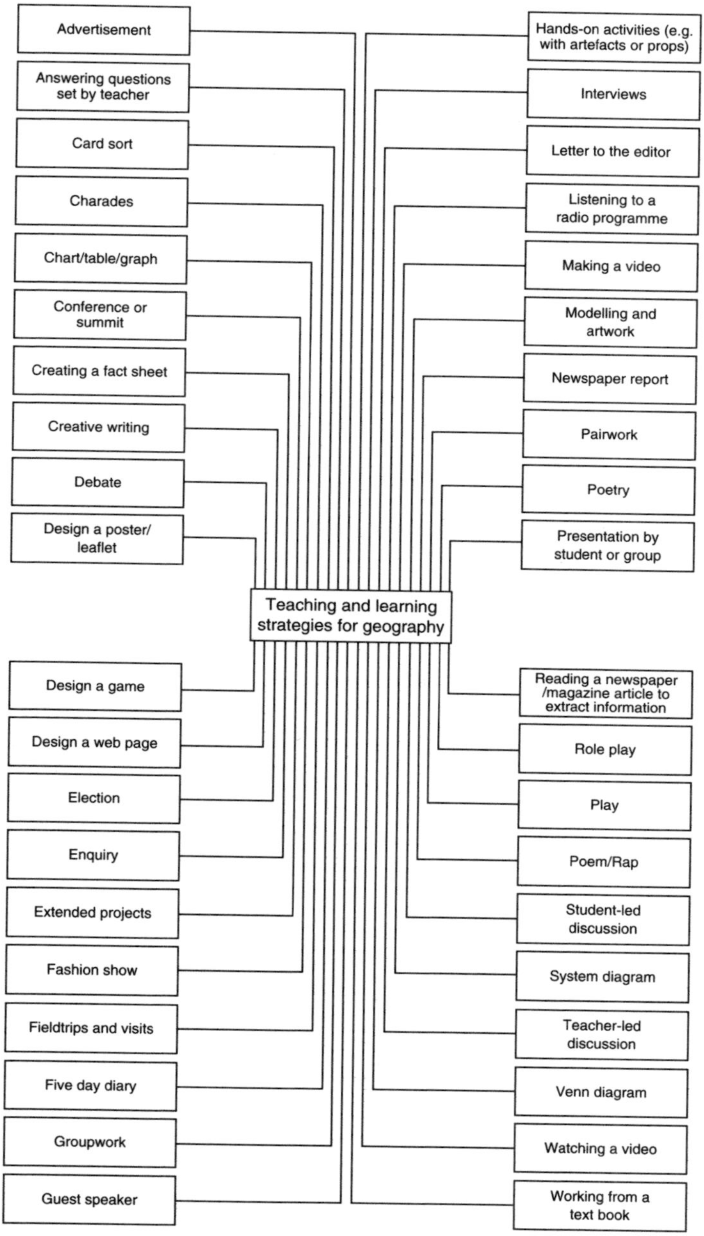

Figure 2.4 Teaching and learning strategies for geography

Task 2.3: Audit your teaching and learning strategies

Cast your eyes over Figure 2.4, considering as you do so the strategies you habitually use and those that are outside your current comfort zone. Write the name of each strategy in the first column below, and add in any strategies you use that are not mentioned in Figure 2.4. Then complete the matrix, placing a tick in the relevant column.

Strategy	Never use	Sometimes use	Frequently use	Often use

Now that you've carried out this audit, what does it suggest about the range of teaching and learning approaches that you currently use? Which student learning preferences do your favoured teaching strategies appeal to? What, if anything, needs to change in the light of these findings? Which parts of this book are going to help you to address these areas? Who can support you as you try to diversify your teaching repertoire?

As you set to work in diversifying your teaching strategies, you may find it helpful first to locate each strategy on the continuum below. The further to the right-hand side of the continuum you place the strategy, the more challenging it is likely to be to implement. Remember, however, that it is good for your own professional practice – and the benefit of your students – to work outside your comfort zone.

←--→

Tried, tested and safe strategies **Innovative/experimental strategies**

The best geography teachers are successful because they are able to, over the course of a unit of study, harness an effective *blend* of teaching and learning approaches that appeals to the widest possible range of students. Effective geography lessons also incorporate extensive *variety* in order to keep students on their toes.

Teachers need to be wary of delivering the same kind of lessons every day simply because they seemed to 'work' with a particular group. For this reason, effective geography teachers experiment, take risks and sometimes make mistakes. This goes with the territory of creative teaching and learning.

Reflection for geography

Any good teacher actively reflects on their lessons and thinks about what they might need to change in the future. The hemisphere of reflection for geography takes things much further by suggesting that a whole suite of reflective approaches needs to be used in order to improve classroom practice. Figure 2.5 gives some examples, and Task 2.4 asks you to get into the spirit of reflection.

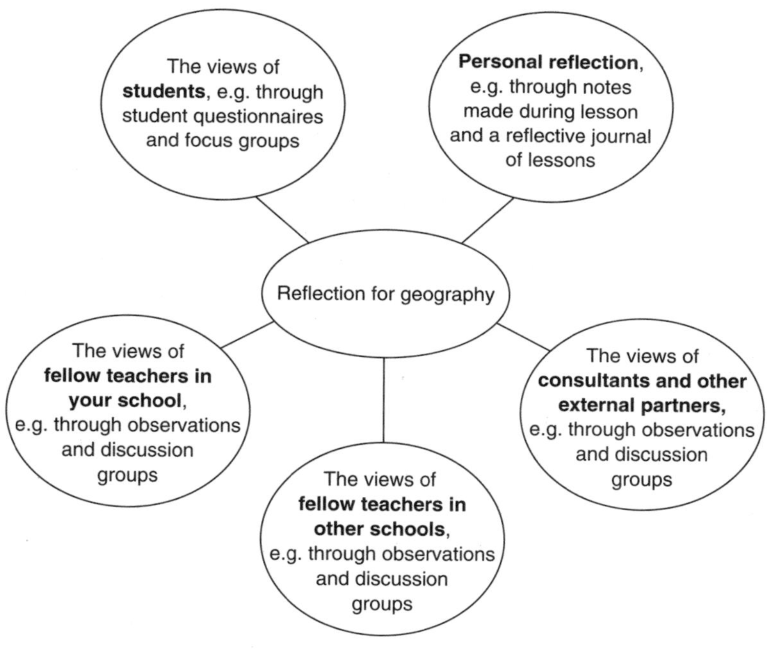

Figure 2.5 Reflection for geography explored

Task 2.4: Reflection for geography

Consider a lesson you taught recently, and consider the following questions:

- What went well in the lesson?
- What did not go so well?
- What did your students think of the lesson? (How do you know this?)
- How would they suggest it be changed next time you teach it?
- What other pieces of information could you gather in order to make judgements about the success of the lesson?
- Who else could help you to reflect on the success of lessons in the future, and how might they be involved?

The key principles of outstanding geography lessons

I've had the pleasure to observe some wonderful examples of inspirational geography teaching over the last few years. It is clear that there are *lots* of thing going on when really good geographical teaching and learning is taking place. It is not just about students being excited by a geographical idea or fact, or about the class having 'fun' in your classroom. Figure 2.6 attempts to provide an aide memoire to guide your thinking about high quality geography lessons. This figure includes many of the principles that Ofsted inspectors are looking for when they make judgements about your lessons. Task 2.5 asks you to consider which of these principles are routinely seen in your own geography lessons. Don't worry that this list seems like a demanding and exhaustive one: the many practical suggestions in this book are designed to help you move towards being a truly expert geography teacher.

The importance of creativity

Creativity is the quest for new ways of thinking and doing. It has key relevance to geography because in order to solve some of the principal geographical conundrums facing the world, we need novel solutions. Just like those making vital decisions about how

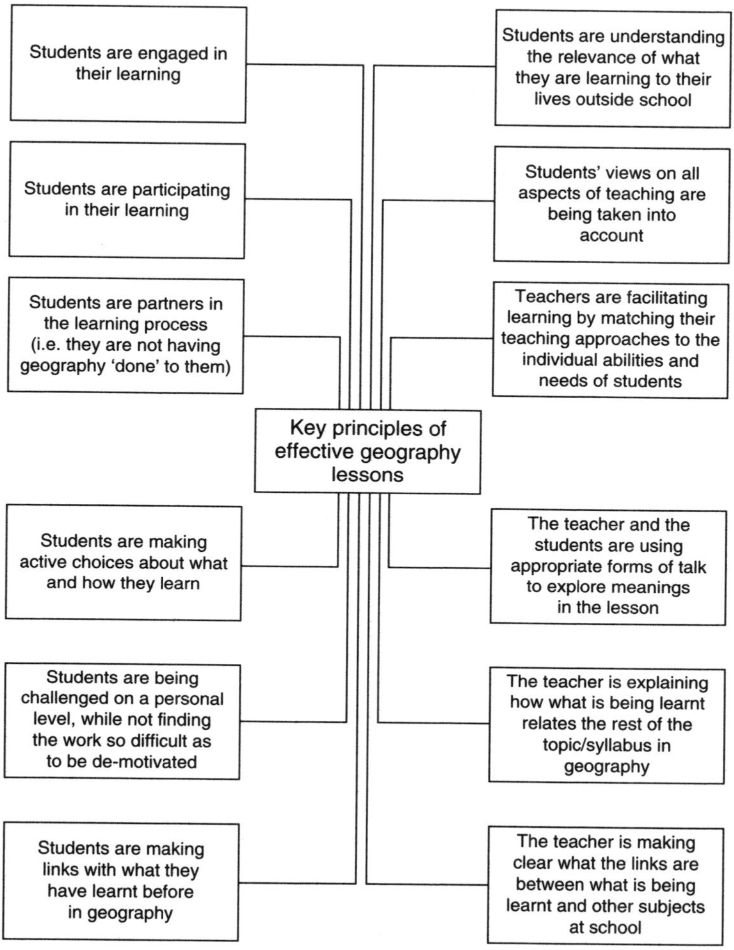

Figure 2.6 Key principles of outstanding geography lessons

Task 2.5: Towards outstanding geography lessons

Study Figure 2.6 that outlines the key principles of outstanding geography lessons. Consider your teaching over the last half-term, and give yourself a score out of 10 for each of the principles listed. Which principles stand out as requiring the most attention? Create a prioritized list of actions that you will need to take to move your lessons towards the 'outstanding' category. Then think about whom in your school can support you as you strive to make your geography lessons outstanding and what they can do to help you.

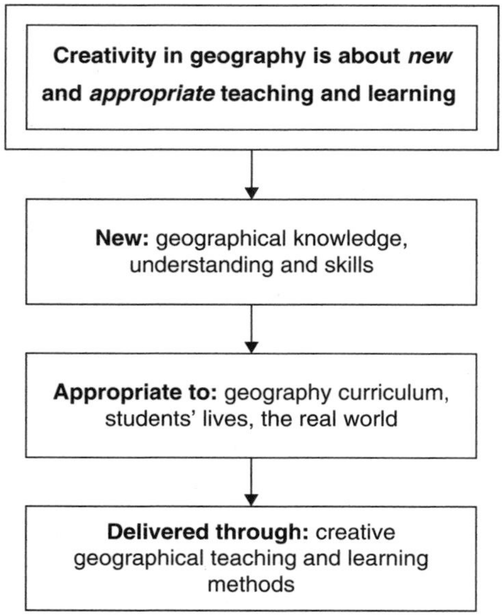

Figure 2.7 Geographical creativity

we will address these global, national and local challenges, your students need to develop their own creative skills. They need a toolkit for creative thoughts and creative action that will help them to pass their exams, to find a job, to become effective employees and to manage life's day-to-day challenges positively.

There is a special kind of creativity that has particular relevance to geography, and Figure 2.7 explores this concept further.

According to this model, creative geography teaching and learning methods help to ensure that students' geographical knowledge, understanding and skills are developed, which has relevance to the geography curriculum, students' lives and the real world. Teachers can, through some targeted teaching and learning methods, help students to develop their own creativity in geography. Throughout this book, there are many examples of how students can utilize creative (i.e. new and appropriate) methods to enhance their geographical learning and develop their creative toolkit.

Furthermore, creativity can be considered a process with eight distinct steps (Figure 2.8) which can be broken down and taught discretely or as a whole. In this way, every student can be enabled to develop the eight steps to creativity. Note that while your

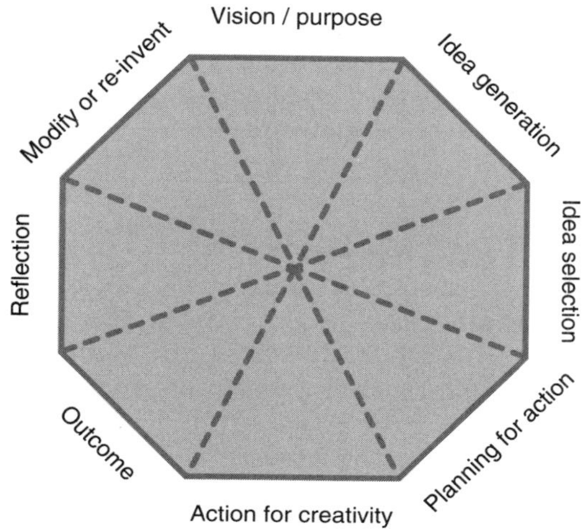

Figure 2.8 The creativity cycle

First published in Best, B., and W. Thomas (2007). *The Creative Teaching & Learning Toolkit*. London: Continuum International Publishing.

Task 2.6: Creativity for learning

Consider the eight steps to creativity shown in Figure 2.8. Think about your teaching over the last couple of weeks, and consider the extent to which you have allowed your students to develop each of the eight steps to creativity. Which steps have you allowed time for and specifically encouraged your students to develop, and which steps have not been targeted? Creativity for learning is often best considered when students have been challenged to solve a particular problem or carry out an enquiry. Draw up a shortlist of the specific steps to creativity that you intend to target in the future. Is there an argument for having a special series of lessons where the eight steps to creativity are worked through with some geographical content? Note that it is likely that your students may be pretty good at the first two steps: being clear about the purpose and then generating possible solutions, but be less good at the remaining six steps. They may need some targeted support in order to develop their competence in these aspects of creativity.

students may be good at coming up with ideas (the first step), they may not be that effective at selecting the most appropriate ideas to implement and then working hard to put these into practice. This can be addressed by specific teaching of these steps, allowing your students to develop their creative repertoire (see Task 2.6).

The ideal geography student?

The result of your outstanding geography teaching is that you will have helped to produce well-rounded students who have excellent geographical knowledge, understanding and skills, and are well placed to play their full part in decisions affecting their lives and those of others, whatever their chosen career. There's no doubt that in order to do this, you'll need to be at your best, but you also need the active support of your students. A fun way of thinking about this is to ask students what the ideal geography student might look like. Give your students an opportunity to draw a cartoon showing their views of what an ideal geography student might look like ,and allow yourself time to do the same (see Task 2.7).

Task 2.7: My ideal geography student

Create your own cartoon to show what your ideal geography student might look like. For example, the cartoon might show the equipment the students might carry with them (in a rucksack perhaps?), the clothing they might wear or the habits of mind of really good geographers (shown through thought bubbles). You may want to look back to your work on Task 2.1 to remind you of some of the key principles underpinning your work. Scan this into the computer, and project it for your students to see, explaining as you do so what each of the factors are. This kind of activity is an ideal way to start the year, to help students to see where their geographical learning is heading. The best time for students to create their own cartoon would be towards the end of their study of the subject, reviewing what they have learned about the qualities of an ideal geography student.

3 Practical classroom matters

Overview

This chapter focuses in detail on the nuts of bolts and lesson planning and 'delivery'. If you've not yet read the opening two chapters setting out the context for the book and the key models that underpin effective geography teaching, now is the time to take a quick look at them. Particular note should be taken of the Four Hemispheres of Geography Teaching and the Creativity Cycle, as the remainder of the book assumes you have a working knowledge of these models. Throughout this chapter, emphasis is placed on practical strategies for the classroom, with tried and tested teaching and learning activities that you can use straight away. If you want additional immediate inspiration for your lessons linked to specific parts of the geography curriculum, you should also look at the 'Lesson stimuli' online at http://education.best.continuumbooks.com.

Planning for effective teaching and learning

The old adage that proper planning prevents poor performance could not be truer for the teaching of such a dynamic subject as geography. The multifaceted nature of the subject and the range of resources that can be employed to bring geography to life mean that careful preparation for learning is essential. It is generally true that the most effective lessons are those that require the most time to set up, so do not shy away from the planning time needed to deliver outstanding geography lessons. Teachers new to the classroom will naturally take some time to build up a bank of highly effective lessons. A certain amount of patience and a willingness to curb your natural desire to try to perfect the art of teaching in the first term will be needed. It will take some time to become the master of your classroom. This leads us to the crucial matters of lesson planning and schemes of work.

★ *Lesson planning and schemes of work*

Every good geography department is rigorous with its planning. While everyday innovation is encouraged, each lesson forms part of a wider learning framework that is set out in lesson plans and the schemes of work that fit these together into the jigsaw of geographical learning. These represent part of your vision for geography and form a constant point of reference for teachers and students – the highest performing departments often sharing the schemes of work with students, on giant mind maps (see page 86), for example.

Your lesson plans should be concise, allow room for innovation and flexibility, and cover the following information:

- Date of lesson
- Duration of lesson
- Learning objectives
- Four-part lesson structure: put learning in context, starter, main teaching and learning, plenary
- Differentiation techniques
- Extension.

This information is best laid out in tabular format as shown in Figure 3.1.

It is important to bear in mind that geographical learning often involves enquiries and topic work that extends over several lessons. It is important to prepare lesson plans for each of these

Date of lesson **Time of lesson**	**Duration of lesson**
Level of group	
Lesson theme	
Learning objectives	
Resources	
Four part lesson structure	
Put the learning in context	
Starter	
Main teaching and learning *(including principal learning episodes)*	
Plenary *More able will do…* *Most students will do…* *Less able will do…*	
Differentiation techniques	
Extension	
Teacher reflection on lesson	

Figure 3.1 Lesson planning

Key stage/ year group	**Topic**	**Sub-topic**	**Length of time**	**Lesson theme**	**Learning objectives**	**Key resources**	**Notes**

Figure 3.2 Schemes of work

lessons to ensure that students are not coasting, and have clear learning objectives for each of the lessons in a sequence.

Your schemes of work should set out learning objectives at a broader scale, outlining for each topic what will be learned and the methods that will be used to aid that learning. Again, a tabular structure is best for schemes of work, as shown in Figure 3.2. Your schemes of work should include a breakdown of each lesson that will be used to cover each subtopic being studied, together with the learning objectives to be covered. They should also include links to other aspects of the syllabus.

Rigorous schemes of work and lesson plans will provide the platform for the delivery of outstanding geography lessons and should serve as a constant reference point throughout the school year. Task 3.1 invites you to think about your schemes of work and lesson plans in more detail.

Task 3.1: Schemes of work and lesson plans explored

Read over the above text about schemes of work and lesson planning. What are the major challenges you face as you prepare schemes of work and lesson plans? What have you tried to do to overcome these? Which parts of this book will help you come to grips with the specific challenges you face? Who else in your school and further afield could support you as you strive to improve your schemes of work and lesson plans?

Specific challenges of different year groups

Learning how to be an outstanding geography teacher will include an acceptance that there are a range of challenges which must be faced to ensure that every lesson engages learners. In addition to the day-to-day challenges you encounter with all the groups you teach – which are explored throughout the book – there exist some challenges that are more or less specific to certain year groups

★ *Key stage 3 challenges (year 7–9; age 11–13)*

Key stage 3 represents an important three-year period because the choices that students make at the end of the key stage determine whether they will continue to study the subject to GCSE level in years 10 and 11. As such, it is vital to show students the full riches of geography during key stage 3 so that the maximum number of students will continue to choose to study the subject through to key stage 4. This is especially important in the light of the declines in the number of students taking geography GCSE in recent years. Some of the other challenges at key stage 3 include:

- The importance of providing a seamless continuation from any geography that has been taught in the primary school – this will be especially challenging where the details of what was taught in the feeder schools are sketchy.
- The need to provide continuity with the content to follow at GCSE level.

- Successfully immersing your students in the culture of the department, which may be quite different to the classroom culture of their primary school and may even be other departments in your school.
- Providing an effective balance between geographical knowledge, understanding and skills, providing the springboard for study at GCSE level.
- Enthusing your students so they see the relevance of geography to their lives.
- Showing your students the fun side to geographical learning.
- Providing previews of what will be learned at GCSE level so students can see where their learning is heading and look forward to that learning.

★ *Key stage 4 challenges (year 10–11; age 14–16)*

Once GCSE study gets into full swing, the two years of study seem to race by. Given the focus on GCSE examination results, key stage 4 represents perhaps the most pivotal period for any geography teacher. Some of the major challenges at key stage 4 include:

- The balance between preparation for exams and the wider enjoyment of the geography syllabus.
- The need to develop geography fieldwork skills as well as classroom knowledge and understanding.
- The pressures of competing subjects which students are taking.
- The pressures that are brought by demands outside the classroom: for example, clubs and other extra-curricular activities, weekend jobs.
- Providing previews of what lies ahead in A-level geography.

Given that the success of your geography department will be largely judged by your GCSE examination results, the need to channel much time and resources into years 10 and 11 is clear.

★ *Key stage 5 challenges (year 12–13; age 17–18)*

If your school has a sixth form, then hopefully enough students will choose geography to form at least one AS/A-level group. For many teachers, working at this level is one of the crowning joys of geography teaching, with enthusiastic students helping you to take the subject to all sorts of exciting places. Some of the major challenges at key stage 5 include the following:

- The balance between preparation for exams and preparation for potential study of geography at university.

- The pressures of other subjects which students are taking.
- The increasing significance of paid part-time work by students outside school.
- The balance between coursework and exam work (depends on the syllabus being studied).
- The need to keep the subject 'fresh' even after five years of study.
- The need to help students develop increasing autonomy as learners, while not losing sight of the key guiding role of teachers in every classroom.

Task 3.2: The challenges of the key stages

Read over the above text about the challenges of different key stages. Which challenges are most relevant to your own circumstances? Are these the same for everyone in your department? What have you tried to do to overcome these challenges? What will be your top three challenges moving forward?

Understanding the needs of individual learners

Now that I have discussed some of the big-picture issues affecting the teaching of geography, the following text explores in detail some of the day-to-day matters that will concern you as you design outstanding learning opportunities. The key principle here is that effective teaching and learning depends on a sound understanding of a range of factors affecting students' learning.

★ *Multiple intelligences*

Much has been written about the topic of multiple intelligences in recent years. They were put on the educational map through the pioneering work of Harvard professor Howard Gardner in his book *Frames of Mind: The Theory of Multiple Intelligences* (New York: Basic Books, 1983). Gardner's theory is simple: he argues that intelligence should not be measured through the traditional measure of IQ but instead should be understood as a much wider concept, encompassing eight 'multiple intelligences' as follows:

- Interpersonal
- Intrapersonal
- Kinaesthetic
- Linguistic

- Logical-mathematical
- Musical
- Naturalist
- Spatial.

Gardner's theory struck a chord with many teachers, and this led to a range of new measures being introduced into schools to catalogue students' intelligence profiles and teach in ways that widened their repertoire. Some of the key points to bear in mind about Gardner's theory and its application in geography classrooms include the following:

- Diagnostic tests aimed at determining students' intelligence profiles can be helpful and generate useful information about a student's all-round abilities.
- Gardner never argued, however, that students' intelligence profiles are fixed; instead they can be seen to constantly change as the student matures.
- Geography provides ample opportunities to develop all the multiple intelligences, but you will need to find some creative ways to nurture some of Gardner's intelligences (music for example, but see page 36 for advice on how to do this).
- The mission of every geography teacher should be to help students to develop *all* their intelligences; students should not be allowed to use a low score for one of the intelligences as an excuse for poor performance in a specific aspect of the geography curriculum as all the intelligences can be developed.
- Although multiple intelligence theory has important implications for geography classrooms, there are pitfalls for the unwary. In particular, schools should not be tempted to go too far down the route of diagnostic testing of multiple intelligences, especially the separation of students according to their intelligence profiles.
- In groupwork, for example, it would be wise to sometimes arrange groupings to ensure that there are students in the group with strengths in a wide range in intelligences. This will ensure diversity in addressing tasks.
- Gardner also considered existential and moral intelligence as potential further intelligences but eventually rejected them. As Gardner's 'intelligences' essentially represent aptitudes in specific domains, there are arguments for retaining them, as indeed there are arguments for adding other additional intelligences to the list. You may find that a student in your class displays an intelligence that does not easily fit with one of the above-mentioned intelligences: for example, a student who is highly creative. As such, be open to adapting Gardner's theory to suit your own circumstances. Remember: it remains a *theory* that has not been rigorously tested.

Learning activities for the multiple intelligences

Specific activities can be used to appeal to the intelligences of the students you teach or to develop their intelligences. They are listed below:

Interpersonal intelligence

- Learning from others
- Working in teams
- Talking to others to share and get answers
- Comparing notes after a study session
- Making use of mentoring
- Teaching others

Intrapersonal intelligence

- Setting goals and targets for learning
- Creating personal interest in the learning
- Taking control of learning
- Carrying out independent learning
- Seeking out the human angle
- Reflecting, writing or discussing what was experienced and the feelings this invoked

Kinaesthetic intelligence

- Learning by doing
- Role play and drama
- Field trips
- Taking action: for example, writing down points or mind mapping
- Making models
- Card sorting exercises
- Moving about while working
- Mental review of learning while doing physical exercise

Linguistic intelligence

- Learning from books, tapes, lectures and presentations
- Writing down questions that need to be answered before starting to learn
- Reading aloud
- After reading a piece of text, summarizing in own words out loud and writing this down
- Putting thoughts into own words
- Brainstorming to organize thoughts into order or to distinguish key points

- Making up crosswords and word puzzles to solve
- Debating and discussing issues
- Presenting what has been learned orally or in writing to another student

Logical-mathematical intelligence

- Listing key points in order and numbering them
- Using a flowchart to express information in easy to follow steps
- Using mind maps
- Using computer spreadsheets
- Using timelines for remembering events
- Analyzing and interpreting data
- Creating and solving problems

Musical intelligence

- Using music to relax before learning
- Studying music that reflects what is being learned
- Reading rhythmically
- Writing a song, jingle, rap or rhyme
- Using musical approaches to memorize key words
- Music can be used for the benefits of all students, and further advice on using music in the classroom is given on page 36.

Naturalistic intelligence

- Learning outdoors: for example, on field trips
- Investigating environmental issues
- Identifying and classifying the natural world
- Reading about nature and the environment
- Listening to guest speakers who are nature specialists
- Devising role-plays with an environmental theme

Spatial intelligence

- Learning from film, video, slides and PowerPoint presentations
- Using mind maps, symbols and diagrams
- Designing a poster with key facts on a topic
- Highlighting key points in different colours
- When reading, visualizing events in mind's eye
- Studying in different settings or areas of the room to gain a different perspective
- Converting information into diagrams or pictures.

Adapted from Best, B., *Accelerated Learning Pocketbook* (Alresford, UK: Management Pocketbooks, 2003).

★ *Emotional intelligence*

Daniel Goleman introduced the concept of emotional intelligence (EI), which builds on Gardner's inter- and intrapersonal intelligences. Its relevance to the geography classroom is that by paying attention to students' EI, you can help them to enter a more resourceful psychological state for learning. The EI or emotional literacy of your students can be *developed,* so it is important to build in ways of promoting EI in your lessons. There are six main components of EI:

- *Self-awareness* – having objectivity about your own feelings and noticing the feelings as they occur.
- *Self-discipline* – being able to motivate oneself and stay on task.
- *Empathy* – being sensitive to the needs and feelings of others and understanding that people are different and have different needs.
- *Persistence* – being able to keep at a task, even if it is challenging.
- *Emotional management* – constructively managing our own feelings and recognizing the useful information that lies behind them.

Studies of Harvard University students have shown that it is those with high EI – not high IQ – who are most successful in their careers. Ideas for teaching EI in the geography classroom include the following:

- Encourage students to monitor their own strengths, weaknesses and progress in geography (see page 56 for an example of a record card on which they can do this).
- Help students to assess their readiness to learn through a traffic lighting system – each student is given three cards marked with a red, amber or green circle. When prompted by the teacher, they hold up the card that best represents how ready they feel to learn. Green means they feel very ready to learn, amber means they may need to some help to feel ready to learn and red means they definitely do not feel ready to learn. The reasons for lack of readiness to learn can be multi-faceted and could include feeling stressed, anxious, tired, hungry, thirsty, angry, and so on. A variety of strategies will need to be used to help students overcome their barriers to learning.
- Encourage students to routinely set their own targets for their geographical learning at a variety of levels. These can include an overall target grade for their GCSE or AS/A-level, a target mark for an end-of-unit test and a target grade for their next piece of written work.

- Reward persistence with praise and effort marks when noted, and try to help make persistence and determination part of the culture of your classroom.
- Help your students to empathize with each other and with people outside school using a variety of techniques: get them to share their worries/concerns about their geography studies; encourage them to learn about other students' strategies for improving in geography; allow them to learn about the life of young people in other, especially poorer, countries to build empathy for the daily struggles of others.
- Emotional wisdom (the ability to use our EI to contribute to our families, our communities and humanity as a whole) is the ultimate goal of teaching for EI. One of the most effective ways that students can learn emotional wisdom is to have it modelled by their teachers.

You can read more about EI in Goleman's seminal book *Emotional Intelligence: Why It Can Matter More Than IQ* (London: Bloomsbury Publishing, 1996).

★ *Learning styles*

Closely related to the concept of multiple intelligences is the notion of learning styles. The use of learning style analyses in schools has become very popular in recent years, with some schools even going as far as grouping students according to whether they are considered visual, auditory or kinaesthetic learners. Some essential things to bear in mind about learning styles in the geography classroom include the following:

- Students should be seen to have a *preferred* learning style rather than having a sole learning style which dominates.
- In reality, every student has a balance of learning preferences and cannot just been seen as learning in one way (e.g. all students must be able to learn through the auditory route to some extent, unless they are deaf, though it may not be their *preferred* learning style).
- Learning preferences are not fixed and can be developed; indeed it could be argued that teachers should do everything in their power to help their students to develop *all* their learning styles so they become more rounded individuals.
- Students should not be allowed to hide behind their preferred learning styles when challenged to learn in a different way. I have heard some students, whose learning 'style' has been diagnosed, shy away from carrying out specific tasks, because they claim they do not learn that way. The reframe needed here is that it may not be their *preferred*

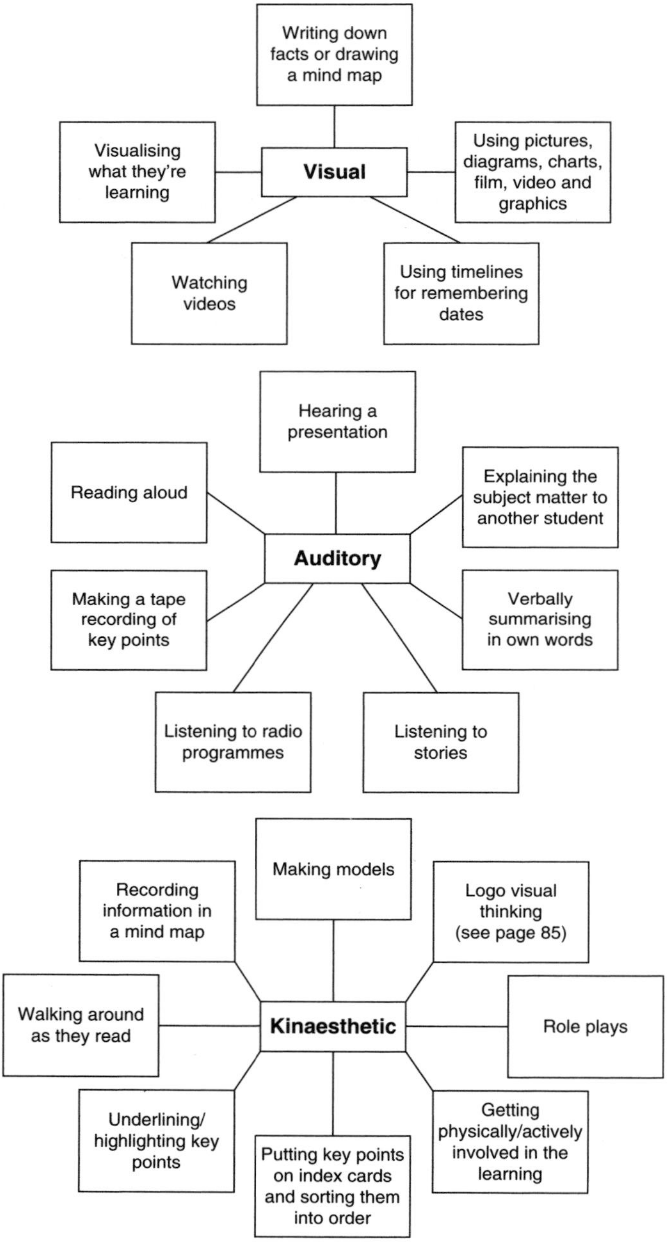

Figure 3.3 Activities for different learning preferences

learning style, but they *are* capable of learning that way. Indeed, with practice it may become a more preferred option.

- Geography by its very nature provides some rich ways of learning using all three routes, and as a teacher, you should provide ample opportunities for students to learn in visual, auditory and kinaesthetic ways (VAK).
- Learning styles are not confined to the VAK trio; learners can also have a preference to learning according to a whole host of other factors, including being wholist/partist, being analytical learners or learning through imagination. A key role of the geography teacher is to identify how they can develop the widest range of learning preferences as possible. Some examples for VAK are given in Figure 3.3.

Task 3.3: Exploring learning preferences and multiple intelligences

Read the text on learning preferences, multiple intelligences and emotional intelligence. For each of the different preferences and intelligences, give yourself a traffic light reading to determine how well you think you cater for each in your classroom as follows:

- Give yourself a green light if you cater for it well.
- Give yourself an amber light if you cater for it quite well.
- Give yourself a red light if you do not cater for it very well.

For those learning preference and multiple intelligences which have a red light, consider how you can be inclusive of these in your classroom, using the ideas presented in the book. Do any of these actions present any contradictions or problems in your setting? Repeat the exercise at the end of the next two terms, and see how the results vary.

Varied classroom approaches

The remainder of this chapter will consider the principal approaches that can be harnessed inside and outside the classroom in order to plan really effective learning experiences. The emphasis throughout is on designing truly engaging and stimulating learning experiences.

★ *Accelerated learning*

Any teacher working in a UK secondary school will be sure to have heard of accelerated learning. Some may even be passionate advocates of the approach, having been on one of Alistair Smith's excellent courses on the subject. There is no doubt that accelerated learning has much to offer in helping to get the most out of your students.

Accelerated learning happens when we teach in way that respects how students' brains learn most effectively. There are three main aspects to accelerated learning:

- Ensuring students are in an appropriate *physiological* state for learning.
- Ensuring students are in an appropriate *psychological* state for learning.
- Using appropriate teaching and learning strategies that promote the most effective learning.

There are close links between accelerated learning and the Four Hemispheres of Geography Teaching (see page 9), as accelerated learning directly addresses both the 'Classroom climate for geography' and the 'Teaching and learning strategies for geography' components.

Whole books have been written about accelerated learning (see below for suggested reading), and this is not the place to go into detail about how to use the approach, but there are some key points to bear in mind when you plan and deliver your geography lessons. Follow the 12-step plan:

1. Ensure your students are in the correct physical state to learn (proper hydration [see box] is important as are room temperature and oxygen levels).
2. Use music in a targeted way to promote learning (see page 36 for details).
3. Help students enter a positive emotional state for learning (e.g. by relaxation exercises).
4. Create a classroom culture that supports learning but makes activities challenging.
5. Develop very good working relationships with your students, and use praise frequently. Get to know them as individuals.
6. Plan inclusive learning activities that respect the full range of learning styles and intelligences, and are accessible to all students.
7. Use the following sequence in lessons:
   Part 1: put the learning in context
   Part 2: starter
   Part 3: main teaching and learning
   Part 4: plenary
8. Allow breaks for light physical activity (e.g. brain gym).
9. Use a very wide variety of teaching methods including thinking skills and visual tools to develop higher order skills.

10. Make learning skills such as mind mapping and memory techniques part of your lesson.
11. Encourage students to review their own progress and set personal goals.
12. Evaluate your lesson in consultation with your students.

Some people have argued that accelerated learning simply represents best practice in the classroom, and I have some sympathy with this view. The leading ambassadors for the subject would say that what marks accelerated learning out from simply good teaching and learning is that accelerated learning takes advantage of recent scientific findings into the brain and how it learns most effectively.

Accelerated learning has been a particular passion of mine for the last ten years, and for more information on accelerated learning, see my *Accelerated Learning Pocketbook* (Alresford: Teachers' Pocketbooks, 2003). A more in-depth reader on the science behind accelerated learning is Alistair Smith's *The Brain's Behind It: New Knowledge about the Brain and Learning* (Stafford: Network Educational Press, 2002). Task 3.4 gets you thinking about how well you embrace the principles of accelerated learning.

WATER, WATER EVERYWHERE

The brain is 90 per cent water, and it has long been recognized that in order to stay mentally alert, we need to drink plenty of water during the day. The reason for the lethargy of some of your students may be that they are dehydrated. For this reason, it is important to allow students to drink water during your lessons. I carried out some action research in my department on water consumption during lessons and found that it brought many benefits to my students. As well as keeping them hydrated, it was empowering for the students to be allowed to bring a drink into their lessons and made them feel more grown up. Contrary to some concerns by staff members, water bottles were not a distraction and quickly just became another part of the classroom furniture alongside pencil cases. The approach which worked best was to have each student bring their own reusable water bottle into lessons, which they had filled up prior to the start of the lesson. If water consumption by students is not yet a feature of your lessons, do something about it this week! If students are prevented from bringing water into lessons because of a school-wide rule prohibiting it, then talk to the rule makers and show them this book. It is one small, but significant, step that all teachers can make.

★ *Using music*

Music should be considered a very helpful tool in promoting geographical learning. Music can be used in a wide range of ways, both to relax and prepare students for learning, and to add an extra dimension to the study of a particular topic. But using music in the geography classroom is not just a matter of putting on the radio, or listening to the latest pop songs to hit the charts; instead, there is a science behind its successful use in the classroom. Effective use of music in the classroom is seen as an integral part of the accelerated learning approach, by preparing students for learning. For more about accelerated learning, see page 33.

Music for relaxation

Music can be used to help relax students so they are in a ready state for learning. It is thought that music can help to stimulate what are called alpha brain waves, which are characteristic of a state of relaxed alertness which is most conducive to learning. The following pieces of music have a regular beat of between 50 and 70 pulses per minute (the same as the human heart at rest) and are ideal relaxers:

- Beethoven, *Violin Concerto in D Major*
- Debussy, *Clair de Lune*
- Enya, most of her work
- Gregorian chant, any piece
- Handel, *Water Music*
- Mozart, *Piano Concerto No. 21*
- Vangelis, *Chariots of Fire* (and much else of their music)
- Vivaldi, *Four Seasons.*

Note that these are just a sample of the many pieces of music that could be used to relax students. It is a good idea to have a chat with your head of music in order to explore some alternatives that students might be familiar with from their music lessons.

If you routinely play relaxing music as students enter the classroom, they will soon get used to this pattern and indeed come to expect it. The playing of music can be combined with a puzzle (e.g. anagram, word search, crossword) on the whiteboard, to help prepare students for learning. Alternatively, music related to the topic being studied could be played at the start of the lesson (see below).

Music to promote geographical learning

Music can further be incorporated into the main part of your lessons in a range of ways. These include:

- Playing music from a country or region being studied: for example, Cuban salsa music, Cajun music (from the Mississippi Delta) – this helps students to get the feel of the culture of the place they are studying.
- Playing traditional tribal music when studying rural communities in less economically developed countries.
- Music to aid memory – it is thought that playing music while a particular topic is being studied can help students to recall information about that topic when the music is recalled.

The question of whether music should be played while students work is an interesting one to explore. If you carry out a survey, you will find out that practically every one of your students works to music while at home. This raises an important question: how natural is it for students to work in silence, as they are expected to do in so many of their lessons? The conclusion I draw is that there is a strong argument for allowing music to be played while students work, at least from time to time. The need to work in silence can, however, be seen as a key skill to acquire, and is something that perhaps needs to be practised, not least because students will have to do so in their examinations. Allowing students to choose the music they listen to during periods of solo work can also be empowering for young people, and can also be used as a reward for good work or behaviour.

Other uses of music

Music can be used in the following additional ways:

- To energize students who may be listless after a long day in the classroom – in this case, upbeat music should be used to lift their spirits.
- To provide breaks – it is good to build in brain breaks into your lessons, and music can be used to help provide relief for students who have been working intensively for a period of time. A variety of musical styles can be used, but the best are those with a distinctive feel which help to provide a sense of transition from one activity to another.
- As part of a 'concert review' at the end of a lesson – turn the lights down, put the music on and display images on the whiteboard pertinent to the topic being studied.

It is just one step further to use not just music but dance in your geography lessons. For more about dance in geography lessons, see page 105.

Think carefully about how you can use music in your classroom – it can become a distinctive feature of your lessons that your students will appreciate and has an important role in aiding the learning process.

Task 3.4: Do you teach accelerated learners?

Accelerated learning has the potential to have a major effect on classroom practice, with multiple benefits for students. Consider how well you currently embrace the accelerated learning agenda in your school, including the use of water and music to aid learning. Which aspects of accelerated learning do you embrace fully, which ones do you partially embrace and which ones do you not currently embrace? Are you skeptical about any of the claims of accelerated learning, and, if so, where can you learn more about these claims in order to help you make an informed decision? Are you aware of anyone in your school who is a passionate advocate of accelerated learning? If so, try to observe some of their lessons to try and learn from them.

★ *Independent learning*

Independent learning is a process through which students develop knowledge, skills and understanding through their own efforts. Independent learning has great value in preparing students for life after school as well as helping to give them the intrinsic motivation to succeed in their geography studies. As such, it has immense value, and great emphasis should be placed on helping your students to become more autonomous learners. As you help your students to become independent learners, bear in mind the following:

- A key principle underpinning independent learning is the notion that students accept personal responsibility for their learning.
- It has many benefits to students, such as:
  - It represents a more adult and realistic approach to learning which reflects lifelong learning models.
  - It encourages flexibility and good decision-making skills.
  - There is a scope for different learning preferences to be accommodated where choice is given over how to access sources of information.
  - It helps students to have greater levels of self-motivation through freedoms and choices.
  - It encourages students to develop self-evaluation skills.
- Independent learning requires a shift in emphasis in your approach as a teacher, as you move to being a facilitator of learning rather than the person at the front of the class managing the learning process.

- Differentiation during independent learning can be achieved by varying levels of teacher support for students – getting the balance right between extensive teacher support and fully independent work can be difficult and requires some trial and error.
- The resource implications need to be carefully thought through, in particular:
  - the need for liaison with library/resource centre staff in relation to information, space and support.
  - students' internet skills: do they need specific training before they can begin?
  - the potential need to reorganize the classroom environment to make it more suitable for a flexible learning set-up.
  - the fact that resources may be available beyond the institution: for example, in the local community. Consideration needs to be given to how they will be accessed.
  - how support materials will be stored and retrieved.
- Special emphasis should be placed on the development of self-evaluation skills – students need to be encouraged to reflect not just on what they have learned but how they have learned it, so they can improve their learning skills.
- Perhaps the best example of independent learning in the geography classroom is enquiry-based learning (see page 76).
- Because it is the predominant method of learning in universities it is vital that students – especially at A-level – have experience of it during their school education.

★ *Developing literacy through geography*

Geography offers some wonderful opportunities to develop literacy through a range of teaching and learning strategies (see box). As such, the subject has a major contribution to make in developing literacy across the curriculum, complementing work being carried out by your English department. In particular, developing literacy in geography enables students to work on the skill of writing with a purpose.

The importance of literacy in subjects like geography has been highlighted by the inclusion of literacy in the key stage 3 strategy. When developing their literacy skills in geography, students should be encouraged to include a distinctive element of geography in their work. In this way, they can be seen be developing their *geographical literacy*.

- The following should be born in mind about developing literacy in geography:
- In order to maximize the development of good literacy skills, SMART targets should be set for the department, which clearly relate to whole school objectives.
- To ensure that your literacy work integrates effectively with that at the whole school level, it is important to liaise with your literacy coordinator, who will be able to provide advice on strategies as well as letting you know the kind of work that is taking place in other departments.
- You should try to tap into the CPD provided on literacy across the curriculum which will help you to spot opportunities and give you lots of ideas for lessons.
- Your literacy work needs to complement work on speaking and listening which is also a critical part of the work of the geography department (see below).
- In order to improve your teaching of geographical literacy, first consider how you currently teach it, and then think about how it could be enhanced through some new actions.

Geography literacy – examples

The following examples show a range of ways in which geography can develop students' literacy skills:

- Letter to the editor – students give their views on a geographical issue.
- Newspaper article – a 300-word concise news article on a geographical topic.
- Magazine feature – a 500-word feature article providing an in-depth focus on a particular theme.
- Diary entry – a day in the life of somebody affected by a geographical issue.
- Poem, rap or song – expressing in a creative way the student's views on a geographical issue.
- Campaign manifesto – outlining what the student will do to tackle a major geographical issue.
- Short story – students prepare a short story that brings to life a geographical issue.

★ *Developing oracy through geography*

Oracy can be defined as listening, speaking and spoken interaction, and the subject of geography has an important role to play in developing students' oracy skills. Oracy is a valuable life skill, and within geography, students have the potential to develop a distinctive form of oracy – geographical oracy.

The development of oracy skills has considerable value in schools and should be carefully documented in your department. Oracy shouldn't be something that 'just happens' in lessons – it should be an integral and explicit part of lesson planning. There is growing evidence that children's learning can be enhanced by facilitating structured talk in the classroom Talking is particularly effective because it helps students to sort out their ideas.

One of the important features of oracy is students' growing awareness of the language appropriate to different audiences, purposes and situations. Students also learn to take turns and listen to others and become proficient at appraising different forms of speech. Oracy skills can be developed in the geography classroom through pairwork, groupwork and whole class teaching.

A particularly important part of *geographical oracy* is active listening. Individuals need to be guided to listen for information and then be given opportunities to respond on an individual, pair or group basis. As the teacher, you have a key role in modelling effective listening: for example, by maintaining eye contact, having positive body language and asking appropriate questions in response to what you have heard.

The teaching of oracy skills should not, of course, be seen as a bolt-on activity. It should be an integral part of every lesson and should be planned for. In order to improve your teaching of geographical oracy, first consider how you currently teach it, and then think about how it could be enhanced through some new strategies.

Geographical oracy – examples

There are many ways in which oracy can be developed in the geography classroom, including the following:

- Debates
- Role plays
- Question and answer sessions
- Listening to radio programmes
- Listening to each others' point of view

★ *Developing numeracy through geography*

Geography has a key role to play in the development of numeracy skills – the ability to understand numbers and calculations. Its inclusion as part of the key stage 3 strategy has emphasized its role in secondary schools.

Numeracy finds a natural home in the geography department because of the need to manipulate number data as part of the study of the subject. The teaching of numeracy within geography lessons should therefore be a seamless part of teaching and learning in the subject. Furthermore, students can be considered to be developing their *geographical numeracy*

It makes sense, for the purposes of whole school auditing, to document the various ways in which numeracy is developed in geographical. You may also wish to include some notes on this in your schemes of work. If you are need of some inspiration for your numeracy work, team up with your whole school numeracy coordinator or the head of maths to try to identify opportunities.

In order to improve your teaching of geographical numeracy, first consider how you currently teach it, and then think about how it could be enhanced through some new actions.

Geographical numeracy – examples

The following examples illustrate some of the many ways in which numeracy can be developed through geography:

- Working out percentages for population data.
- Looking at climate data and plotting climate graphs.
- Drawing pie charts of employment patterns.
- Working out river flows from gauging station data.
- Looking at economic data from cities across the world.

★ *Using role play*

- Role play is an important tool in the armoury of every geographer teacher, but is often underused, or only used on special occasions. Role play is especially valuable because it gets students actively involved in their learning and forces them to engage with the subject matter in a focused way. Some issues to bear in mind about role play are as follows:

- Role play should be seamlessly integrated into your lessons and should not be seen as students as a bolt on or a special treat.
- Role play can be used when students are arranged in pairs, small groups or working as a whole class.
- Role play is an ideal way for students to be made aware of the differing views of people on contentious issues. This helps students to see points of view that they may not habitually share, and perhaps enables them to change their view when presented with additional information.
- Role play does need careful setting up and monitoring by the teacher to ensure that students are benefiting from it. Without teacher intervention, it can easily become an exercise in who can speak the loudest.
- It can be fun, from time to time, to allow students to dress up in appropriate costume, or to bring in a prop, when involved in role-play work.
- When using role play, links can be made to other areas of the curriculum such as English (developing oracy skills) and drama (the performance side of role play). It may even be possible to organize joint lessons with teachers in these departments.
- Extensive support and preparation should be used with students who are engaged in role play; otherwise it can become an exercise in guesswork. For example, students can prepare or be provided with a fact sheet that helps them to understand the point of view of the person they are asked to take the part of.
- Role play provides good opportunities for the teacher to take part in the learning by acting out a part. There are links here with the 'hot-seating' approach where the teacher takes the role of expert and students ask questions to explore an issue.

★ *Personalizing learning*

The best geography departments have always had a focus on making learning *personally relevant* to all students, and they carried out much work in this critically important area long before the government's national 'personalized learning' agenda was implemented. Really successful teaching in geography – as it is in every subject – centres on the unique, individual needs, skills and abilities of learners and how these can be respected and nurtured. Thankfully, the days of 'teaching to the middle' are now long gone, replaced by a mission to inspire *individuals*.

Personalizing learning in geography has much in common with the drive to personalize learning opportunities in other subject disciplines, sharing specific strategies and tools used in these disciplines. The overall aim is to ensure that every student achieves their potential in geography.

The overall aim of personalized learning is to ensure that students achieve their potential by working in a collaborative learning environment. It is different from *individualized learning,* where learners work in isolation from each other. Some of the main considerations for personalizing learning in geography include:

- An acceptance that personalization is not a new concept and simply builds upon what the best teachers already do – it is a mission to make best practice universal and should be seen as a banner for tackling a whole host of disparate issues which are important to the work of teachers.
- The 'inner core' of the government's personalization framework – which encompasses assessment for learning (see page 53), effective teaching and learning, and curriculum entitlement and choice – has most relevance to classroom geography teaching.
- The most significant area of focus to achieve personalisation is effective teaching and learning – much thought should be given to how lessons can be made personally relevant to students.
- Respect for the *learning preferences* of individuals – for example, visual, auditory, wholist, analytical etc.
- An awareness that learning outcomes often need to vary from one individual to another, to ensure personalization.
- The provision of *choices* in geographical learning enhances personalization and gives students more ownership of their learning. These choices can be linked to the nature of tasks, the speed with which they are carried out and the method of presentation, among other factors.
- Personalization may be harder to achieve for very able students or those who struggle to access the curriculum for a range of reasons – such groups will need special attention.
- Geography teachers can establish links with a wide range of partners in order to enhance personalization for students – these include outside speakers, parents/carers and the local education authority.

Differentiation can be seen to be part of the personalization agenda, since it concerns how material is presented to learners or the kinds of tasks that are required of them.

Geographical learning can be differentiated in the following ways:

- By breadth of learning – more able students can cope with more depth.
- By depth of learning – more able students can cope with more breadth.
- By pace of learning – more able students can cope with more pace.
- By task – tasks of varying difficulty can be set for different students.
- By learning preference – for example, visual, auditory or kinaesthetic.
- By outcome – for example, higher-ability students will produce more. detailed/higher-level work, or will have additional learning outcomes to the less able.
- By stimulus material – such as by using newspaper articles instead of teacher prepared worksheets.
- By teacher support – more support is given to students of lower ability.
- By gender – different learning activities are offered which reflect the personalities and interests of boys and girls.

The above factors can be varied by frequency as well as magnitude to cater for the widest range of students as possible. It is possible to identify several groups of students for which differentiation is especially necessary:

- Very able students (see page 46)
- Students of lower ability
- Students with a special educational need
- Students with dual exceptionality (e.g. very able and with a special educational need)

Making careful choices as to how learning is differentiated in your classroom will help ensure that you have embraced the principles of personalization. Differentiation strategies need to be built into lesson planning so they are not seen as a bolt on; instead they should be considered an integral component of any lesson. A good way of achieving this is by using the 'more able, most, less able' model (as shown on page 23), whereby different learning outcomes are expected of different student groups. A variation on this theme is to consider what *all* students will do, what *some* (more able students) will do and what a *few* (very able students) will do.

The following text on differentiation for more gifted and talented (more able) students shows how differentiation can be achieved within a mixed-ability classroom. The four principles of differentiation for more able students outlined below can also be used as a tool for differentiating learning for other student groups (e.g. less able students) by, for example, reducing the difficulty of the task challenge. Note that using these principles, some teachers plan their lessons 'from the top', by outlining what gifted and talented students will do and how the learning will be modified for less able students. This approach raises expectations for all.

Differentiating for gifted and talented students

The government has championed the education of so-called gifted and talented (G&T) students (see box) over the last decade through extensive targeted funding and new school systems. In most schools, G&T students represent the top 5–10 per cent of students in each year group, so we are not talking about the elite which you might teach once or twice in your career. It is likely that your department will have been asked to identify students who are more able in geography, so that these students can be added to the school's G&T register (which your school is required to submit to government as part of the annual school census every year). Even if you have not been asked to identify a G&T cohort in geography in this way, you should do it because it will help to ensure that learning is personalized according to their needs.

Gifted and talented students defined

Gifted students – those who achieve (or have the ability to) significantly above average, compared with students in their year group at your school, in one or more of the National Curriculum subjects other than art, performing arts and physical education.

Talented students – those who achieve (or have the ability to) significantly above average, compared with students in their year group at your school, in art, performing arts and physical education.

What does a gifted student in geography actually look like? Some of the characteristics of more able students in geography are contained in the box.

Characteristics of a gifted student in geography

- Is comfortable using maps and has a well-developed sense of how a map relates to real features on the ground.
- Has an innate passion for the outdoors and is inspired by natural landscapes.
- Has a deep fascination for landforms and how they are made.
- Is able to empathize with the views of others, even on controversial subjects.
- Without prompting, is capable of asking geographically relevant questions about places, photographs or cartoons.
- Has a natural facility with fieldwork equipment.
- Has an understanding of how values and attitudes can affect how people think about an issue.

Note that a student does not have to display all of these characteristics to be considered gifted in geography.

An excellent departmental exercise is to write what your team understands by gifted and talented geographers in your school. This is the best starting point for any work to target this student group.

Research has indicated that more able students in geography thrive in lessons where:

- There is ample breadth and depth to learning.
- The stimulus materials are challenging.
- The task challenge is high.
- The pace of learning is purposeful.
- There is much independent learning.

These can be seen as the five principles underpinning differentiation for more able students.

Task 3.5: Inspiring gifted and talented students in geography

Consider the five bullets points above which describe the kind of lessons in which G&T students thrive. Then think about a lesson you taught recently and reflect on the degree to which you addressed each of the factors listed. Give yourself a rating of very good, good, adequate or poor for each of the four factors. A tool for recording this information is given below. For anything you rated adequately or poorly, consider what you will need to do in order to improve things next time. An extension exercise could involve observing a fellow teacher at work and each person scoring the lesson as above, then comparing the results.

Lesson title	Breadth/depth of learning	Challenging stimulus materials	High task challenge	Purposeful pace	Independent learning

The box gives an example of how learning can be differentiated for more able students in the context of a mixed ability classroom. This is likely to be the most common situation in which students are found in your school.

It is important, when considering the needs of more able students, to be on the lookout for able underachievers – namely, those who have high ability but fail to reach their potential for a variety of reasons.

Differentiated learning in the mixed-ability classroom

Lesson theme: Project-based learning

Learning through projects is undergoing something of a renaissance in schools, thanks to the relaxation of the curriculum at key stages 2 and 3 and the government's mission to encourage more creative ways of engaging children in their learning. Project-based learning centres on pupils driving learning and making their own creative breakthroughs, rather than working slavishly towards learning objectives set by the teacher. The range of topics that can be explored through projects is limitless, and we include here just one worked example based on the theme of waste minimization in schools.

Guidance notes

In a classroom context, a project is a learning activity that achieves a focused objective against a timescale, usually having the following characteristics:

- A clear end result.
- A fixed timescale.
- Involving a team of pupils.
- Involving little practice or rehearsal.
- Involving a change.

Project-based learning works especially well when it takes place in small groups and is appropriate for both mixed-ability or ability-based groupings. If mixed-ability groupings are used, then different stimulus materials or activities of varying difficulty need to be allocated within the group, as shown in Table 3.1. If ability-based groups are used, then different groups can be given stimulus materials and/or activities appropriate to their level. Ability-based groups can also be given different questions within the main theme of the project in order to achieve differentiation, and to ensure that each child is stimulated and stretched appropriately.

During learning of this sort, you need to be prepared to hold back as a teacher, and let your pupils take the lead, as well as being flexible and allowing them to leave your classroom in order to carry out surveys, interview people or conduct further research.

Project brief

Key question → How can we reduce waste at our school?

In groups of 4 to 6, your task is to recommend ways in which waste can be reduced at our school. At the end of four lessons, you will be asked to present your suggestions to the rest of the class. These suggestions need to be practical and realistic. All members of the group must take part in the presentation.

Table 3.1 Differentiation guideline

TYPE OF DIFFERENTIATION	**FOUNDATION ACTIVITIES** **Aimed mainly at less able pupils**	**INTERMEDIATE ACTIVITIES** **Aimed mainly at more able pupils (top 50 per cent of those in class)**	**HIGH-LEVEL ACTIVITIES** **Aimed mainly at very able pupils (top 10 per cent of those in class)**
Stimulus material	Pupils given a basic resource pack, including one newspaper clipping, one web address and a leaflet about recycling. Pupils to consult resource pack to extract information on waste and how it can be reduced.	In addition to the basic resource pack, pupils are given an intermediate resource list in order to carry out further investigations. The list could include sections in books, newspaper articles and websites. Pupils to consult resource pack to extract information on waste and how it can be reduced.	In addition to the basic and resource pack and intermediate list, pupils are given a list of 'open ended', more advanced research ideas, including: - newspaper websites to search and navigate - telephone number of waste management department of local council - the suggestion for a visit to the school library In addition, pupils are asked to find and list their own sources of research on this topic, including books and websites. Pupils to consult resource pack to extract information on waste and how it can be reduced.

Task challenge	Pupils given three questions: Q1. What different types of waste are produced in our school? Q2. How much waste is produced in our school, and how it is disposed of? Q3. How can our waste be reduced? The following suggestions for activities are made to pupils: take a tour of the school, do a survey, interview someone, ask for specialist advice, find out which option is most popular.	Pupils given four questions (Q1–3, plus another) Q4. Find out what other schools are doing to reduce waste. What lessons can we learn from this for our school? Three of the activity suggestions in the previous cell are provided.	Pupils given five questions (Q1–4, plus another) Q5. Investigate the wider issues around waste management in the United Kingdom and across the world. What lessons can we learn from this for our school? Pupils are not given any suggestions for activities.
Pace	Each pupil or pair in the group is assigned one of the above questions to focus on. All findings will be collated by the group prior to the presentation.	Each pupil or pair in the group is assigned one of the questions 1–3 to focus on. The group will discuss their findings, and then all address question 4 as a group prior to the presentation.	Each pupil or pair is assigned two of the questions 1–3 to focus on. The group will discuss their findings, and then all address questions 4 and 5 as a group prior to the presentation.
Depth/breadth	Pupils identify three of the main types of school waste (e.g. paper, metal, plastic, food) and suggest at least two ways that it can be reduced.	Pupils identify four or more types of school waste and three ways of reducing it, including ideas from other schools.	Pupils identify multiple types and ways of reducing school waste, including how it is tackled within and beyond schools in the United Kingdom and overseas.
Independent learning	Pupils work with frequent reference to the teacher's verbal and written guidance on next steps. Pupils make some choices about learning.	Pupils work with infrequent reference to the teacher. Pupils make frequent choices about learning.	Pupils work with very infrequent reference to the teacher, including extended periods in the school library or at home. Pupils make very frequent choices about learning.

Extension

Project-based learning can be extended in a range of ways. The amount of time given over to the project can be extended to encourage even more breadth and depth, or to allow pupils to interact with a range of external experts including speakers and visitors inside or beyond the school. Pupils who are interested in this topic can be encouraged to take the 'project' further in their own time – for example, by setting up a school recycling group in order to bring about real change in their school.

Gifted and talented students represent just one student group that you need to cater for in your lessons. Other groups include less able students and students with special educational needs. Each of these groups has particular needs which need to be catered to in the classroom (see Task 3.6).

Task 3.6: Differentiation in practice

Identify three different student groups that need to be differentiated for in the classroom. For each group, explain how you can differentiate learning for them for a specific lesson? How successful are these differentiation techniques? What are the challenges of differentiating learning for diverse student groups, and how can these be best overcome? What common principles underpin your differentiation strategies?

★ *Pairwork*

Pairwork is a very effective tool for classroom learning and should be used frequently. The fact that it is universally popular with students and is guaranteed to get them talking make it a firm friend of the geography teacher. Some of the key things to bear in mind about pairwork are as follows:

- Make sure that students get to work with different partners during the course of the year, rather than always working with the same one.
- Pairwork involving students of similar ability and students of different ability levels both have their merits – ensure there are opportunities for both in your classroom.
- Ensure you vary the gender mix in the pairs you set up (boys and girls often flock together when given the choice).

- It is important to keep a close eye on students working in pairs to ensure they are on task, as pairwork provides the potential for-off task activity.
- Give a clear time limit for pairwork to keep the work of the pair focused.

★ *Groupwork*

Groupwork is another very valuable and popular tool for learning and should be a familiar feature of your lessons. Key points to bear in mind with groupwork include the following:

- As with pairwork, vary the specific composition of groupings, and set up groups consisting of students of similar ability and also mixed ability.
- Ensure a good gender mix in the groups you set up.
- To maximize student involvement, ensure that each student is assigned a specific role during groupwork (e.g. scribe, discussion leader, timekeeper, etc).
- Be vigilant to the off-task discussion which can happen with groupwork.
- Give a clear time limit for groupwork to keep the work of the group focused.
- Groupwork provides superb opportunities for logovisual thinking (see page 85).

Task 3.7: Pairwork and groupwork compared

Read the text on pairwork and groupwork, and then complete the table below, which considers the pros and cons of each.

	Advantages	**Disadvantages**
Pairwork		
Groupwork		

What are the implications of this table for your teaching in future? How can you introduce more pair- and groupwork into your lessons, while at the same time ensuring that learning outcomes are met? What do you think the balance should be of pairwork to groupwork?

★ *Assessment for learning*

What else can assessment be for? The government's recent drive to promote assessment for learning (AfL) has rightly encouraged teachers to find ways of ensuring that assessment is used as a careful tool to promote learning in the geography classroom.

Assessment for learning is about using evidence and dialogue to identify where students are in their learning, where they need to go and how best to get there. AfL can be seen as a major part of the government's drive to personalize learning. As part of AfL, four strands can be identified:

- *Questioning* – the need to put more thought into high-quality open question that promote higher order thinking (see also page 81).
- *Feedback through marking* – where teachers encourage students to expand upon and show understanding of what they have learned.
- *Peer and self-assessment* – students need to know what success looks like and should be taught the skills of feedback and self-evaluation.
- *The formative use of summative tests* – where students are involved in reflective activities to review their work and prepare appropriate strategies.

Tips to get the most out of AfL in the geography classroom include:

- Take account of the five big principles of assessment for learning (see box) as you plan and deliver lessons.
- Ensure that when starting a unit of study, students know what they are expected to learn.
- Use a blend of formative and summative assessment, but find ways to maximize the formative assessment strategies used in your classroom. Remember that formative assessment is not intended to seek information to assign grades and instead seeks to get feedback on what students know so that teaching can be modified to help them learn.
- Use standard and stretch targets for individuals and groups to encourage high performance in tests and examinations.
- Always provide advice on how students can improve when marking work, making it clear what they need to do to reach to the next level.
- Provide various ways of assessing what your students have learned, in order to respect their learning preferences, such as written tests, verbal quizzes, question and answer sessions with visual stimulus etc.
- Make displays which show examples of students' work at a variety of levels/grades, annotated to illustrate how the individual student has reached a particular level.
- Encourage your students to look at each others' marked work so they can see further examples of work at a variety of levels.
- When your students have become familiar with how you mark their work, provide them with a mark scheme, and get them to mark their own work. If a student can do this properly, they will have a firm grasp of what they need to do to improve their marks next time.

- Get your students to redo selected pieces of work, striving to gain the next level/grade up when they do so.
- Help your students to record the marks and comments they receive by issuing them with a record card (see Figure 3.4). This concise summary of their progress can help to keep track of their performance, strengths and weaknesses in a very systematic way. It can also provide the background information for students to speak about their performance at student review meetings, with parents in attendance (see page 106).

The five big principles of assessment for learning

- The provision of effective feedback to students.
- The active involvement of students in their own learning.
- Adjusting teaching to take account of the results of assessment.
- Recognition of the profound influence assessment has on the motivation and self-esteem of pupils, both of which are critical influences on learning.
- The need for students to be able to assess themselves and understand how to improve.

Assessment for learning methods

A range of methods should be used to assess students' learning and help them to improve their geographical knowledge and skills. They include:

- Teacher marking of work
- Peer marking of work
- Self marking of work
- End of unit tests
- Quizzes
- Multiple choice questions
- Past papers
- Electronic voting
- Video diary
- Reflective learning log
- Diary

The best way to achieve effective assessment for learning is to blend as many of these methods as possible into your lessons, to cater for the widest range of learning preferences. Students need to be introduced to the language of assessment for learning so they can learn how to mark work themselves: for example, by being introduced to criteria mark schemes.

Name:

Form:

Geography teacher:

Figure 3.4 Student record card

RECORD OF MARKS

Piece of work																
Date																
Mark/ grade																

Student comments on marks

(continued)

TARGETS

Date target set ______________________
Target ______________________
Date target met ______________________

Date target set ______________________
Target ______________________
Date target met ______________________

Date target set ______________________
Target ______________________
Date target met ______________________

Date target set ______________________
Target ______________________
Date target met ______________________

Date target set ______________________
Target ______________________
Date target met ______________________

Date target set ______________________
Target ______________________
Date target met ______________________

Date target set ______________________
Target ______________________
Date target met ______________________

Date target set ______________________
Target ______________________
Date target met ______________________

Date target set ______________________
Target ______________________
Date target met ______________________

Date target set ______________________
Target ______________________
Date target met ______________________

Figure 3.4 continued

TEACHER COMMENTS FROM REPORTS

> **Task 3.8: Assessment for learning strategies**
>
> What strategies have you used to achieve assessment for learning? Which strategies have been most effective, and which have been not so effective? To widen your repertoire, find out what a geography teacher in a nearby school does to achieve assessment for learning and observe them at work. This is an especially valuable activity because all too often we ignore what other teachers in neighbouring schools are doing to tackle some of the very same challenges we are wrestling with.

★ *Fieldwork*

Fieldwork represents one of the principal joys of geography teaching. The ability to extend learning beyond the classroom into a range of outdoor settings provides excitement, a change of scene and the opportunity for young people to be inspired by the world around them. The chance to go outdoors appeals to most students whose learning is so frequently confined to the four walls of their classrooms. Fieldwork also allows students to develop some specific geographical skills – such as map reading, using compasses and the ability to read the physical landscape – that will live with them for life. Although in recent years, health and safety concerns have eroded some teachers' confidence in taking children outdoors, the campaign for real world learning has served to re-ignite interest in such activities as fieldwork and helped to cement them as part of the rich tapestry of learning opportunities to which all students should be entitled.

Do not forget that your school grounds provide additional opportunities for geography fieldwork. In addition to fieldwork in the outdoors, geographical learning can take place in a range of off-site locations such as visitor centres, power stations, recycling centres and museums.

Health and safety matters

We've all heard the familiar moans about the so-called health and safety police, but the nature of geography fieldwork – which is often carried out in dangerous or hazardous locations – means that we cannot afford to be complacent. It is quite literally a life and death matter, with on average at least one student a year being killed or seriously injured while on a school geography excursion. In the context of geography fieldwork, the following points need to be stressed:

- Every geography fieldtrip should be risk assessed in order to assess safe working practices and the 'control measures' that may need to be implemented to make work for students safe. Risk assessment centres on two factors: the *severity* of the risk and the *likelihood of it happening*.
- Before every excursion into the field (note that this, of course, also encompasses urban geography: cities can be as dangerous as the countryside, especially if students are not experienced in such environments), a brief health and safety briefing should be issued. This should highlight the key risks and the ways in which students can stay safe.
- There are some particular danger points when it comes to geographical fieldwork that are linked to physical features of the landscape – obvious examples include students working at the top (trip and slip hazards) or foot (danger of falling objects) of steep cliffs, working on unstable slopes and near to or in rivers.
- Special equipment should, of course, be used to help reduce risks while out in the field – including high visibility vests, safety spectacles, hard hats, wellington boots/hiking boots and life vests for aquatic environments. However, these can lead to complacency as the user can begin to feel 'invulnerable' when wearing certain equipment.
- It is easy to let health and safety matters to become so routine that students begin to switch off – try to bring them to life with real stories of how people have been injured in particular circumstances, or by asking students to identify the risks themselves.
- Most important of all, do not allow those who often joke about 'elf and safety' undermine the seriousness of the health and safety matters underpinning all your geography fieldwork. Complacency and light heartedness are real risks in themselves, as this is when people's guard is let down.
- It makes sense to build health and safety into your fieldwork policy and to devise a motto to use with students along the lines of 'we enjoy fieldwork; and we carry it out safely'.
- The purpose of health and safety measures are to assess risks and carry out control measures to mitigate these risks. They are *not* about wrapping children in cotton wool and preventing them from doing all things which are potentially hazardous or bring with them a certain level of inherent risk. Geography fieldwork can and often is moderately hazardous – as is venturing into the great outdoors for any other reason – and this needs to be accepted by staff, students and their parents. We cannot eliminate all the risks in life.

Measurements using specialized equipment

Geography allows students to use some specialized equipment in order to gather data on such things as temperature, wind speed, river flow, slope angle and so on. Taking these measurements brings students into contact with a range of equipment which with they may not be very familiar – in some cases they will never have seen, let alone used, some of the equipment that is utilized. When using such equipment bear in mind the following:

- Students need the opportunity to practise their skills in using such equipment, and it is important to do this *before* they are actually out in the field location gathering the all-important data.
- The school grounds can provide an ideal location for students to practise their skills in using specialist equipment, making their mistakes there rather than in the field proper and gaining the all-important experience that will enable them be proficient field geographers when the time comes.
- Students should be taught to respect geography fieldwork equipment in the same way as they respect science equipment.
- To develop their proficiency in using fieldwork equipment, nothing is better than you as their teacher actually demonstrating one to one or in small groups how particular pieces of equipment work, drawing attention to pitfalls along the way.

Questionnaires

Questionnaires are a very valuable tool in the armoury of geographers and have special relevance during fieldwork. They can help to gather data on topics that can be difficult to sample in other ways, such as people's travelling patterns, shopping habits and opinions on local issues. However, the key to effective questionnaires lies in their proper *design*, as poorly designed questionnaires can confuse interviewees and produce a weak data set. Some of the issues to bear in mind when designing and conducting questionnaires include the following:

- Consider *data presentation* at the stage of designing your questionnaires – be clear what sorts of responses will give you data that can be graphed, charted or mapped.
- Avoid too many questions that yield responses that are simply 'yes' or 'no' as these over-simplistic questions often serve to uncover important detail that is then lost from the data set.
- Questionnaires can be completed face to face, but can also be done through mailed question sheets, or those left in public places for later collection.
- When carrying out face-to-face questionnaires, keep the number of questions to between five and ten so that you keep the interest of your interviewees.

- Explain briefly to interviewees what your questionnaire is about, be polite and do remember to thank all those who answer your questions – you may need their help again in the future!

Fieldsketching

Fieldsketching is an important but often neglected skill in geography, and it is important to find every opportunity for your students to practise their field-sketching skills in a variety of different settings. The basic skills of fieldsketching can be taught by using the view from the classroom window, though students should be given the chance to hone their skills in a range of authentic settings, sketching a range of subjects from the realms of human and physical geography. Although good fieldsketching does require a firm grasp of some artistic skills, any student can be helped to become a better field-sketcher. Some of the ground-rules for fieldsketching include the following:

- Draw the sketch inside a frame and put the labels outside it – use neat lines to outline buildings, landforms and other things that can be seen, without using shading – a fieldsketch is not meant to be a polished piece of art.
- Begin by getting students to concentrate on the main things that can be seen without worrying about the intricate details – these can follow when more experience has been gained.
- Effective labels are as important as a good outline sketch of what can be seen. Keep the labels reasonably concise, but include details which help to bring to life what can be seen.
- Get students to think about *why* they are completing a fieldsketch and the kinds of subjects and labels that are of relevance to other geographers and laypeople.
- It takes a lot of practice to become a good fieldsketcher – try to help your students to develop this skill by providing good 'model' fieldsketches that you or other students have made, then give plenty of opportunities for students to develop their own competency.

Creative approaches to fieldwork

There is a danger that geography fieldwork can become a little regimented once all the standard methods of data collection and topics have been exhausted. Try to spice up geography fieldwork by including a range of creative approaches, such as:

- Investigating an unconventional or whacky topic: for example, what effect will granddad Simpson's new greenhouse have on his street?

- Getting students to make their own sampling equipment: for example, vegetation quadrats using coat hangers.
- Asking students to devise their own fieldwork programme once they have become experienced enough to do so.

You should aim to always keep geography fresh and maintain the interest of your students through these approaches.

Task 3.9: Fieldwork explored

Consider the fieldwork opportunities you offer your students. Imagine that you have to explain to an Ofsted inspector in concise terms how you use fieldwork to promote geographical learning. Prepare a 300-word statement that will form the basis of your explanation. Give yourself an Ofsted rating for how well you are doing (you would find it helpful to talk to a trained Ofsted inspector at this stage if there is one on your staff). How can you develop fieldwork in future? Are there any resource implications? If so, which of the funding sources in Chapter 5 might prove helpful?

★ *ICT in geography*

The development of Information and Communication Technology (ICT) in schools has heralded an exciting new era for teaching and learning in geography. The subject of geography is ideally placed to take advantage of a very wide range of ICT equipment and software. The increasing number of computers found in classrooms may mean that you are teaching at least one of your geography lessons in a computer suite, or at the very least can easily book such a room, or a bank of laptops.

The range of ICT tools and internet resources available to enhance geographical learning is bewildering – not to mention the wealth of software programmes that can enrich your school's virtual learning environment – and includes:

- Videos (see case study on page 116)
- Smart boards
- Global positioning systems
- Satellite navigation systems
- Mobile phones
- Digital cameras

- Sound recordings
- Voting pads
- Video conferencing
- Online blogs and Twitter sites
- Social networking sites

It is important to issue some basic guidelines to your students on good practice for ICT use, especially concerning the use of the internet (see page 66). These may be issued at the whole school level, but should be adapted to serve the needs of the geography department with its specific ICT tools and approaches. In particular, students need to respect the equipment they are using and understand the purpose of using specific ICT tools so that their time is not wasted, and the tools are not abused.

Some of the main tools and approaches for using ICT in the geography classroom are highlighted below.

Virtual learning environments

Virtual learning environments (VLEs) are computer-based systems for supporting teaching and learning that are created and maintained by schools. They now provide the backbone for much of the learning content that schools make available to students. They typically work over the internet and include a range of tools and content that complement face to face teaching. Most schools now have quite sophisticated virtual learning environments, and there are many ways in which geography can make its mark on a VLE, including the following:

- Notes to accompany the taught syllabus for each year group
- PowerPoint presentations, from lessons and as follow-up material
- Links to popular geography websites
- Students' animations
- Examples of students' work at a variety of levels, to show what others need to do to reach a particular level
- Career advice for budding geographers
- Geography in the news – information on events around the world with a geographical theme, with links to find out more
- A glossary of geography keywords

In order to keep your school's VLE up to date with geography content, somebody in your department needs to be made responsible for passing updates to the school's VLE manager (typically the ICT manager). However, everybody on the geography team has a role to play in providing content, and the named person should be seen as the VLE coordinator.

VLEs can be used in very sophisticated ways as assessment tools, by the provision of tests, quizzes and past papers – all of which can be completed online by students and their marks fed back to them, following teacher appraisal. In order to harness the maximum benefit from your VLE, it is advisable to work closely with the senior ICT staff in your school. They will be aware of far more ways to utilize the VLE than you and can help you to create state-of-the-art content that will inspire and enthuse students.

Harnessing the potential of the internet

There is no doubt that the internet has enormous potential to promote effective learning in geography. However, it also has the potential to hinder learning and allow students to become side-tracked from the topics being studied. The following 'golden rules' for internet use in geography will help your students to gain the maximum benefit from this exciting learning resource:

- The school's general rules on internet use should be observed at all times: for example, regarding visiting inappropriate sites.
- There should always be a clear focus for internet use – students should never simply be 'let loose' on the web to conduct random searches.
- Surfing the web using the full resources of the Google search engine can be very time consuming and can easily lead students into educational dead ends. A clear time limit should be placed on doing such general internet surfing, and appropriate warnings given to students about the potential for their time to be wasted.
- The school's VLE is a great place to filter the best geography websites and provide links to these and a short description of the content. Page 70 gives details of a student activity that can generate suitable material, and of course, as a teacher, you can upload details of your top picks.
- Some schools choose to restrict access to a selection of websites that are uploaded in full to the school's intranet. While this denies students the vast search facilities of Google, it does ensure that they only access high-quality educational sites.
- Students need to be trained to differentiate between websites of different quality. In particular, they need to learn to recognize the difference between official sites giving large amounts of useful information and unofficial ones, often set up by an individual and of dubious educational value. With no quality control governing the internet, students can easily assume that everything they read on the web is true and of

the same quality. A good example is the comparison between the National Hurricane Centre's website (see page 152) and several amateur hurricane-related sites which are full of adverts, incomplete links and out-of-date information. The key here is to encourage students to become discerning internet users. You could even issue a good practice guide for students on using websites.

- The internet is a great place to publish students' work – sample written answers, fieldsketches, charts and diagrams, animations and videos can all be uploaded to the geography area of the school's VLE for use by other students. The fact that the content can be accessed at home means that students' learning can easily be extended beyond the school day.
- Some of the best sites to visit have been set up by fellow geography teachers – juicy geography being a classic example (see page 150).

YouTube as an educational resource

The ever popular site YouTube (www.youtube.com) can be a very valuable teaching resource if used judiciously. There are literally tens of thousands of video clips which are suitable for use in geography classrooms. One of many advantages of YouTube is the way in which it brings you right up close to the action by being filmed by somebody on the spot. Some examples of using YouTube include:

- Analysis of weather phenomena: tornadoes, hurricanes, cloud patterns.
- Studying natural hazards such as earthquakes, volcanoes and tsunamis.
- Looking at what various cities have to offer the resident and the visitor.
- Considering the impact of leisure pursuits on the natural environment.

YouTube is increasingly also the place to go to find educational videos which have been posted by fellow geography teachers or by people working in universities. Just one example of this is an excellent video that explains the geographical seasons which can seen at www.youtube.com/watch?v=taHTA7S_JGk, and includes professional sounding audio as well as top-notch optics. There are also many very fine video clips and PowerPoint presentations that can be used to good effect in starter episodes of lessons.

When using YouTube, there are some obvious pitfalls to be wary of, not least the vast number of trashy videos that have been posted. One way round this is to filter out a selection of the best and include links to these on the school's VLE, thereby cutting down on internet 'clutter' and wasted searches.

Mobile phones in the geography classroom

We are used to hearing about inappropriate uses of mobile phones in schools, but how about using them for some *appropriate* uses too? It is important that we help students to recognize that their phones can be valuable tools for learning, as well as communication devices. Here are some ideas to try out with your classes:

- Ask your students to prepare a **mind map** showing the various ways in which mobile phones can be used to help them learn. The main branches are likely to include mention of telephone calls/texts to find things out, visits to educational content on the internet, and the taking and receiving of photos or moving footage.
- Get your students to take some **photographs** around the school grounds through their mobiles and have them label these up with suitable annotations, on computer or by hand after printing. Make sure that there are some mobiles on hand for students to use in case they don't have their own (unlikely today, but you don't want to make any student feel left out). A class project could see a photo montage created presenting an overview of an important geographical issue – such as environmental quality across the school or community.
- Film some **interviews** about important local geographical issues – these might be with other students, staff or members of the community (perhaps an MP or business leader). These can be later uploaded to the school's VLE, together with some analysis of what has been said. Those carrying out the interviews will need to give their permission before the interviews are posted online. The interviews can form part of a wider piece of work – an enquiry perhaps – into a wider issue
- Instead of using computers to access the **internet**, try getting your students to use their mobiles instead, to illustrate a learning point or as part of some research. You may want to allow this in small groups at one time only, using departmental phones that you can set filters on.
- The recent increase in the amount of **news footage** taken with mobiles – especially that taken from disaster zones before film crews arrive – hints at a new era when footage shot by the general public is entering the mainstream of broadcasting. Get your students to consider the pros and cons of geographical news coverage captured by

mobile phone. In what types of situations would it be helpful, and when might it be a hindrance? What are the dangers in trying to maintain accuracy and impartiality in broadcasting such footage? Could it eventually lead to the end of most news film crews?

- Some of the **GPS mapping functions** of the latest generation of mobile phones make them valuable tools for geographical work involving places and people's relationship to those places. The use of direction-finding software provides just one example of how mobile phones are already changing the way people are taking advantage of the new technology, and this in turn is changing the way they interact with the world. Could these new devices actually be producing 'lazy geographers'?

These approaches to using mobile phones are dependent on students being able to bring their own phones into lessons. If your school is one of the small number that do not allow mobiles to be brought in by students, then you may need to talk to the decision-makers about the rationale for this, now that the value of mobiles as tools for learning has been clearly demonstrated. Perhaps your department could even become the test bed for illustrating the value of mobile phones in the classroom?

The above examples suggest that getting a small number of mobiles for your department seems like a very sensible idea, now that they are such ubiquitous consumer items. Because they now can be bought so cheaply, this shouldn't break your departmental piggy bank!

26 ideas for using ICT in geography lessons

While most of the ideas below will render material which is suitable for uploading to the school's VLE, some ideas are especially suitable, and these are indicated in the text.

1. Provide the caption
Students are shown an image taken from a website and asked to provide a caption that conveys the geographical meaning of the image.

2. What happened next?
Students are shown a short video clip on a geographical theme and are challenged to guess what happened next. Good examples are natural hazard videos.

3. Which country is this?
Students are shown a series of images taken in a country and are asked to identify the name of the country in question. Clues can be provided by including photos of familiar landmarks or buildings. This exercise can be made more challenging by showing students an unconventional image of the country: for example, a smart residential part of a city in an economically less-developed country.

4. Photospot
Students take photos with a digital camera in the local community to illustrate geographical topics (e.g. landforms, features of the urban landscape), which are then annotated with appropriate labels using a drawing program.

5. Videoclip
Students make a short video that illustrates a particular geographical issue which is played to the other students in the group who have to describe and explain what the issue is.

6. Website review
Students are allocated a geographical website and have to produce a 500-word review of the site, assessing its strengths and weaknesses. They complete the exercise by giving the site a star rating out of five. The reviews can be uploaded to the school's VLE to help signpost students to suitable websites which will help their study of geography. See also activity 18.

7. True or false?
Students are given a series of geographical statements and are challenged to visit appropriate websites in order to determine whether they are true or false.

8. Design a website
Using a simple website template, students are given the job of designing a basic website which explores a suitable topic in geography. They can use the Google image search engine to find appropriate images to include in their website.

9. Environmental quality
Students go out into the community armed with digital cameras in order to gather evidence about the environmental quality of the local settlement, both positive and negative. The litter hotspots activity outlined below represents just one component of environmental quality. The images are compiled into a PowerPoint presentation to be shown to other students in the group. An extension activity would be to select the best examples to be shown to town/city councillors in order to spark efforts to improve local environmental quality. The litter hotspots

activity challenges students to find the worse places for litter in their community and take photos to record their location.

10. Spot the difference

Two images are taken of the same place on different days, and students are asked to spot the differences and suggest reasons for these. The images should support a geographical topic of some sort (e.g. people shopping on a high street, the sky complete with clouds, river flow conditions).

11. YouTube top five

Students are given a range of YouTube videos to review and are asked to compile a top five in terms of their value for geographical learning. The top-rated sites can then be added to the school's VLE.

12. Label the photo

Students are given a series of geographically themed photos and a bank of labels. Using a drawing package, they are asked to put the correct labels on the photos on the right places.

13. Odd one out

Four photographs are projected onto a screen, and students are challenged to guess which is the odd one out. The images are selected by the teacher to illustrate a particular geographical topic.

14. News broadcast

Students film a news broadcast with a script they have written themselves on a geographical theme. Natural hazards or environmental issues are a particularly suitable topic for such news broadcasts. The broadcasts are shown to the rest of the group, and the best examples can be uploaded to the school's VLE.

15. Interview with an expert

Students film an interview with a local expert on a geographical topic. This person could be a businessperson, scientist or charity worker. The broadcasts are shown to the rest of the group, and again, the best examples can be uploaded to the school's VLE.

16. Students' views

Students film short sequences explaining the views of individual students on a geographical topic: for example, the building of a new supermarket or bypass. The sequences are shown to the rest of the class before a group vote is carried out to determine the views of the class on whether the development should go ahead. A selection can be uploaded to the school's VLE.

17. Hotspots

Students head out with digital cameras into the local community to find out where the geographical hotspots are and the reasons for these. Photos are taken which are then shared with local councillors in an attempt to improve the situation in the community. This could include litter hotspots and can also be adapted for other local issues such as pedestrian hotspots and parking problems.

18. Website reviews again

Over the course of two lessons and homework time, students are given five geography-related websites to review. They are asked to review the sites for:

- the ease of navigation
- the quality of images and other graphic information
- the quality of the geographical information

A template for doing this is shown in Figure 3.5. Different websites are given to different students in the group, and the top rated sites can be added to the school's VLE to build up the number of weblinks to suitable sites.

19. Animations

Students are challenged to produce short animations on a geographical theme using a simple animation package. These could range from animations which show the dynamics of the weather to a model of the growth of urban areas. Inspiration can be gained by studying some of the excellent YouTube animations of a geographical nature. Again, the best can be uploaded to the school's VLE to act as revision tools for other students.

20. Webcam central

In pairs, students are directed to a webcam site that records geography-related content. They are asked to rate out of ten the value of the site in terms of its appeal to geography students, giving reasons. Students then use PowerPoint to prepare a presentation of the good and bad features of the webcams (labelled photos work well), and the best webcam sites can then be selected for uploading to the school's VLE. Some interesting websites include those showing traffic movements in cities, river flow conditions, and images of people playing and relaxing on beaches.

21. BBC iPlayer top picks

Students are challenged to find five programmes on BBC iPlayer which are of use to geography students. A short presentation to the rest of the class justifying their choices is the prelude to a selection of videos being used throughout the course of the year when the appropriate content is studied. This is an example of an ICT-related activity which can save time for the teacher as the students are locating suitable material for later classroom use.

22. Wikipedia entry

Students are asked to write an article on a chosen geographical topic in the style of a Wikipedia entry (Wikipedia is a free internet-based encyclopedia written by the online community – available at www.wikipedia.org). The spirit of Wikipedia entries is that they are concise, accurate and free of bias. This task will require students to understand the topic in question and explain it in a jargon-free way to a non-specialist audience. Students can include in their article visuals they have made themselves as well as graphics sourced from the internet.

23. A room with a view

Students take a photograph through their bedroom window, download it into a computer drawing program and add labels to show any pertinent geographical features. These can relate to urban or rural issues as dictated by the view through the window. Students print out the labelled photo and share it by pinning it to a large board, allowing others to learn about the geographical features visible through their bedroom window.

24. Draw a diagram

Students are challenged to draw a geographical diagram of their choice on a computer drawing package. The diagram can be sourced from a textbook or the students' notes (not the internet). The diagram should be carefully labelled to make it intelligible to a layperson.

25. Communicating with the world

Students are asked to find an online pen-friend in a less economically developed country and email them about the geography of their home area. There are some excellent sites moderated by adults which can be used to locate suitable pen-friends, which you should use to ensure your students' internet safety. Some very meaningful correspondence has resulted from this type of email pen-friending, which has even resulted in some exciting student exchanges to the far corners of the world. One of the best sites is extensive and well-established www.epals.com, which offers many geographical topics as well as resources to guide students through the communication process.

26. What's your view?

A debate is held into a controversial issue in geography. Then, using computer activated voting units, students register their views which are displayed on the screen. A student on each side of the argument is then asked to justify their views, and the class then votes again, with the potential for their opinions now to have changed due to the justifications given.

Some excellent guidance on using ICT in geography has been produced by the Department for Education and Schools in the form of a CD-ROM which contains worked examples of how ICT can be used in diverse classroom settings. A printed guide to the subject,

Website address		
Date reviewed		
	Positive features	**Negative features**
Could include reference to reliability of site, how old it is, how up to date the information is, attractiveness of site etc.		
Ease of navigation		
The quality of images		
Quality of geographical information		
Star rating /5		

Figure 3.5 Website review

part of the ICT Across the Curriculum initiative, can also be accessed at http://nationalstrategies.standards.dcsf.gov.uk/node/96022.

Geographical information systems

Geographical information systems (GIS) are sophisticated digital tools that allow the user to see various layers of geography information for a specific portion of the planet. The role of geographical information systems is so significant that a whole sub-branch of geography – geographical information science – is now devoted to the study of the subject.

For many, GIS is only just starting to be introduced into geography lessons, but in the more advanced schools, it is already proving to be a powerful tool for learning. Key pointers for GIS are as follows:

- The ability to understand a GIS depends partly on students' map-reading skills, so it is important to address this aspect of your students' geography competence before starting any work on the more complex world of GIS.
- GIS has the potential to touch many areas of the geography curriculum, as well as breathing new life into mapwork. For example, studies of urban development can be illuminated by looking at bus routes, the location of local services and traffic flows.
- Many of the packages available are quite complex to navigate around, so it is wise to select a program which is designed with young people

in mind. A program which is designed to be easily navigated by even GIS novices is the Ordnance Survey's Mapzone (see below).

- GIS is in use today in a wide range of public and private-sector organizations in fields such as urban planning, marketing, economic development, business planning, resource exploration, defence operations, conservation and environmental impact assessment. It is important that students understand the real-life applications of GIS and the people that use GIS as a tool as part of their job.
- An excellent online introduction to GIS is available at http://mapzone.ordnancesurvey.co.uk/mapzone/index.html. It includes a real-life decision-making exercise which shows students how GIS can be used in an authentic setting.

The value of GIS in schools can be demonstrated by the fact that Ofsted has identified that some of the best teaching using ICT in schools comes in the form of GIS-related work.

Task 3.10: Using ICT in your lessons

Study the text on ICT on the preceding pages. Identify five new teaching and learning strategies using ICT that you intend to use in the next half-term. You may find it helpful to talk to your ICT manager if there are technical issues to address for your chosen methods. After you have used them, assess how successful they were, then choose another five strategies for the next half-term and repeat the exercise. Present the results of your work to other members of your department (perhaps using a mini PowerPoint presentation), and ask for their feedback on their favourite ICT methods.

★ *Coursework*

Coursework has traditionally provided a significant proportion of the marks available for GCSE and A-level examinations. This, in turn, has led to students carrying out an element of fieldwork. The recent changes to coursework, however, have weakened its position and reduced the impact of fieldwork on the overall make-up of examinations.

The phasing out of coursework in GSCE and A-levels does not mean that project work which was previously categorized as coursework can no longer be carried out. There is a very strong argument for including at least one long enquiry-type project (see below) at both GCSE and A-level, which results in a lengthy report. In particular getting your students used to the discipline of producing lengthy and carefully structured reports is a very useful lifeskill.

The production of coursework and project-related reports has many benefits. It has a way of galvanizing students into producing high-quality work, and it is likely that in your school some of the best work ever carried out by geography students has been on coursework and project-related reports.

Given appropriate support, students are often highly motivated by extended projects, as they can gain a high degree of ownership of the learning as they work their way through the different stages of a project. They also generally take a great deal of pride in producing a polished and well-presented report. Note that there are now few other subjects (if any) which allow students to work on extended projects of this sort, despite it being an important life skill.

★ *Geographical enquiry*

Geographical enquiries are one of the most distinctive features of the teaching of the subject. They allow students to work through a series of learning steps at their own pace, making new discoveries about the subject matter as they do so. Geographical enquiries typically follow a six-stage process beginning with the posing of the enquiry question and ending with an evaluation of the work done (Figure 3.6).

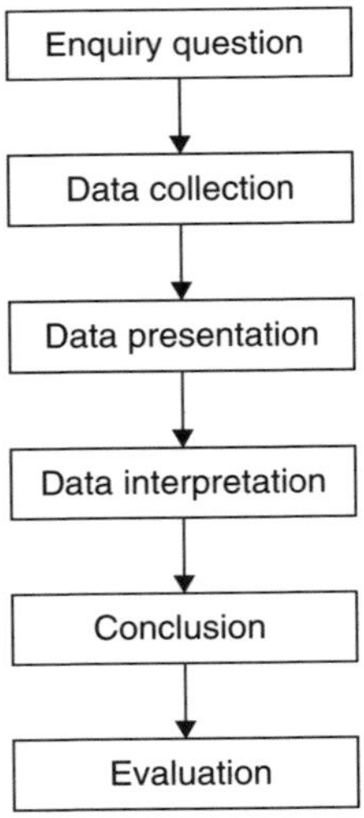

Figure 3.6 The route to geographical enquiry

EXAMPLE ENQUIRY

The following worked example of an enquiry illustrates how students can follow the enquiry sequence while studying a specific topic.

Enquiry question/introduction: should a wind turbine be built on a windy hill?
Data collection: students should collect the following data – the views of the turbine company; opinions of local people; photographs of the site to be annotated with the turbine in place; data on effects of turbines on wildlife, including bird strike rates.
Data presentation: to include annotated photographs of in situ turbine; views of local people and effects on local wildlife presented in pie charts, bar charts and line graphs; facts and figures from the turbine company presented in an easily understood graphic format.
Data interpretation: text description and explanation of what the graphs, charts and photographs presented show.
Conclusion: overall cost-benefit analysis of whether the turbine should be built.
Evaluation: in which the students review their work, pointing out strengths and weaknesses and highlighting areas for improvement.

Other Classic Enquiry Topics

The following enquiry questions can provide the starting point for some stimulating lessons. In some places, specific place names have been inserted where there are many alternatives that could be used. In general, the more local the topic of the enquiry, the better, as it gives it most relevance to students' lives.

- Should the proposed new supermarket be built on the outskirts of town?
- Should a new bypass be constructed to ease traffic congestion in the centre of town?
- Should the number of visitors to the tourist honeypot site of Malham be restricted in order to safeguard the site?
- Should a new oilfield be opened up in the North Sea?
- Should commercial whaling be allowed to go ahead now that stocks of some whales have recovered?
- Should the government provide a grant for a new call centre to be built on a brownfield site on the edge of the city?
- Should new sea defences be built to protect vulnerable villages on the north Norfolk coast?

- Should Britain reduce further its carbon dioxide emissions to respond to the challenge of global warming?
- Should the proposed housing development be allowed to go ahead on the edge of the floodplain of the river Severn, near Gloucester?

The lesson stimuli on the accompanying website also contain many ideal starting points for enquiries.

You should build many enquiries into your geography lessons. Students should be familiar with their structure and the skills needed to carry out each part of the enquiry successfully. The skills of enquiry are valuable life skills in themselves and can be used throughout a student's life to help them solve problems.

Enquiries are also highly suitable for being the subject of student presentations as they generate visually stimulating material as well as having a high level of geographical content. Students should be given the chance to prepare PowerPoint presentations of their enquiries where possible, and encouraged to include charts and photographs which help bring the topic to life.

The enquiry-based approach is ideal to give your students an extended piece of work to be worked on for a number of lessons to develop their independent working skills. Once students are engaged in such an enquiry, the role of the teacher shifts from being the main orchestrator of learning – to being the person who assists individuals as they work through the tasks – at their own pace. The enquiry-based approach allows students to ask deep questions about the subject matter and carry out their own real-life data gathering. As such, it has sometimes been called 'real world' learning. The approach places great emphasis on students taking ownership of their learning, and it fits well with the current drive to put students at the heart of the learning process. It is an excellent example of independent learning (see page 38).

The enquiry will lead to the production of a high-quality report which the students can be proud of, and which can serve as a template for report writing in students' wider lives once they have left school. The report can be of a variety of lengths as determined by the teacher, ranging from concise reports of a few pages in length to more extensive reports which explore the topic in considerable detail.

Task 3.11: Using enquiries in your classroom

Think about the range of geographical enquiries you offer your students. Which ones work best? Try to identify why they are successful. Use these principles to plan a new enquiry which is designed to really stretch students' thinking. You may find it helpful to look back to the text on gifted and talented students (page 46). Discuss your plans with the other members of your department and get their feedback before starting the new enquiry. When you have completed the enquiry, ask your students for their feedback on how much they enjoyed it and how much they feel they learned from it.

★ *Thinking skills*

Geography has a special role to play in the development of so-called thinking skills. This is due in part to the nature of the subject and also the publication of some excellent resources to support the teaching of thinking skills, most notably *Thinking Through Geography* and *More Thinking Through Geography* publications (Cambridge: Chris Kington Publishing, 1998 and 2000).

Thinking skills are skills that promote reflection and more incisive thinking, enabling learners to know 'how' as well as 'what', thereby helping them learn how to learn. The key stage 3 strategy included specific mention of five categories of thinking skills which were embedded in the National Curriculum (see box). This has led to an enhanced place for thinking skills in the curriculum. Note the inclusion of a specific strand covering enquiry skills; enquiry-based learning is a key part of any geography curriculum (see page 76).

National Curriculum thinking skills

- Information processing skills
  These enable learners to:
  - Locate and collect relevant information
  - Sort, classify, sequence, compare and contrast
  - Analyse part/whole relationships
- Reasoning skills
  These enable learners to:
  - Give reasons for opinions and actions
  - Draw inferences and make deductions

- Use precise language to explain what they think
- Make judgements and decisions informed by reasons or evidence
- Enquiry skills
  These enable learners to:
  - Ask relevant questions
  - Pose and define problems
  - Plan what to do and how to research
  - Predict outcomes and anticipate consequences
  - Test conclusions and improve ideas
- Creative thinking skills
  These enable learners to:
  - Generate and extend ideas
  - Suggest hypotheses
  - Apply imagination
  - Look for alternative innovative outcomes
- Evaluation skills
  These enable learners to:
  - Evaluate information
  - Judge the value of what they read, hear and do
  - Develop criteria for judging the value of their own and others' work or ideas
  - Have confidence in their own judgements.

The following should be born in mind about thinking skills in geography:

- Thinking in geography comes in many types and forms, and all these types of thinking can be developed and improved through specific exercises.
- Thinking needs to be *practised* as much as possible as this is only way to improve the quality of thinking taking place in geography classrooms – in short, you need to find *time* for thinking skills.
- Students need to be taught the language of thinking so they can understand what thinking in geography is about and how they can do it more effectively.
- Thinking is best taught where it is infused into geography content, rather than taught as a specific skill.
- There are distinctive ways of thinking in geography which are different to those in other subject disciplines – explain these modes of thinking to your students so they can gain an impression of the distinctive modes of thought in the subject.

- You need to model effective thinking as a geography teacher, for example, by pointing out through an audible commentary how you are thinking about geographical issues and coming to the conclusions you are making.

An essential principle in the teaching of thinking skills is the need to move your students from lower to higher-order thinking. A simple model, devised in the 1950s by US psychologist Benjamin Bloom, helps to illustrate the different levels of thinking – it is now known as 'Bloom's taxonomy'. Bloom actually called his hierarchy 'a taxonomy of educational objectives in the cognitive domain', and he devised it as a way of classifying educational goals, showing how learning can be deepened by using higher-order thinking skills. Figure 3.7 suggests prompt questions that can be used to develop each of the thinking levels for specific and general topics. Figure 3.8, Bloom's learning rose, goes further by suggesting keywords for each thinking level and examples of tasks that can be done at each level.

Some criticisms of Bloom's taxonomy have centred on the belief that the levels are not hierarchical, or that the lower three levels are and upper three are not. However, Bloom's taxonomy has been very influential and remains a cornerstone of pedagogical theory. It will serve as a key reference point as you strive to move your students from lower- to higher-order thinking.

Thinking type	Specific prompt question	General prompt questions
Evaluation	Should we all recycle our household waste?	Which is the best solution? How easy was that?
Synthesis	What conclusions can you draw from your previous answers about waste recycling?	What does this all add up to? What are the main conclusions?
Analysis	For three types of waste explain how each is recycled and the benefits this brings	How much harder was that than the last time we did it? What are the reasons for the shift in position?
Application	What kind of waste is most easily recycled?	How could we use that in another way to help our learning? How can you take advantage of that to address this problem?
Comprehension	Compare the benefits of recycling waste	Explain how that works? What are the results of the experiment?
Knowledge	What are the benefits of recycling household waste?	What facts do you know about that? What were the main points made by the interviewee?

Figure 3.7 Questions to develop thinking

A key part of the thinking skills approach concerns so-called metacognition or thinking about thinking. Metacognition has been shown to be particularly effective in getting students to think more incisively and can easily be built into review periods in lessons. Metacognition typically happens at the end of a unit of work or lesson. The kind of questions that should be asked during metacognitive reflections include:

- Why did we do it that way?
- What were we thinking when we did it?
- Did this help us to answer the question?
- What other things did we have in mind when we were thinking about the question?
- How might we do things better next time?
- What have we learned from this exercise?

Metacognition represents a high-level thinking skill and equates best to the 'evaluate' level of Bloom's taxonomy. The very valuable nature of metacognition demands that we strive to find ways

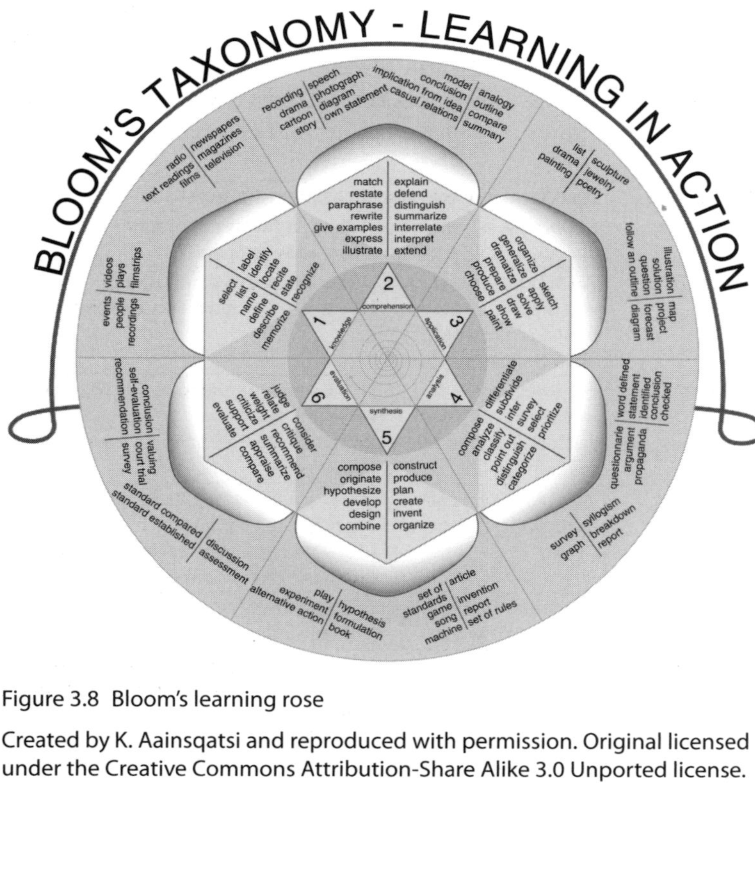

Figure 3.8 Bloom's learning rose

Metacognition in practice

A year 9 class was studying a unit of work on earthquakes, which contrasted their effects on more and less economically developed countries. At the end of the unit, the students were asked to engage in a metacognitive reflection on the unit of work they had studied which focused on the type of thinking they had carried out at different periods of the study unit. The teacher chose three distinct tasks that were carried out by the students and asked them to record for each the kind of thinking that they were doing and how this helped them to do the task. The students were also challenged to think about how they could have approached the task differently through alternative types of thinking and whether this would have helped them to do the task any better. After writing their answers down, a whole class discussion took place, with the teacher writing some of the students' responses in a grid on the whiteboard. A final task asked students to consider what they had learned from the exercise about their thinking and how this might help them in their future geographical studies.

Task 3.12: Thinking skills explored

Study the text on thinking skills, paying close attention to the text on Bloom's taxonomy. Then think about your last week of teaching, and consider the opportunities you gave students to use the various thinking levels in Bloom's taxonomy, completing the table as you do so.

Thinking type	**Examples of opportunities provided**
Knowledge	
Comprehension	
Application	
Analysis	
Synthesis	
Evaluation	

It is likely that there will be more opportunities to develop the lower-thinking levels, even though it is the higher levels of thinking that really stretch students. Consider what you can do to include more higher-level thinking in your lessons. Which prompt questions can you use to help elicit higher-level thinking?

TASC

TASC stands for Thinking Actively in a Social Context and is a way of approaching learning using a problem-solving wheel. The brainchild of Belle Wallace, TASC has recently been introduced into secondary schools following several years of highly successful use in the primary sector. The TASC approach has much merit, and it is well worth devoting some lessons to using the approach with your students. One of the key benefits of TASC is that it encourages students to ask relevant questions about learning and also teaches the cross-curricular skills of problem-solving in a highly structured way. Students who have been introduced to TASC are better equipped to become effective problem-solvers in the real world, as well as in their lessons. There is a substantial body of research backing up the benefits of using TASC in the classroom, and it is a strategy that is well worth investigating. Courses are run on the topic across the country, and an online version of TASC is available at www.tascwheel.com, with extensive support materials. TASC has special relevance to geography lessons, with their emphasis on enquiry skills and extensive requirement for problem-solving (Fig. 3.9).

Figure 3.9 The TASC problem-solving wheel

Copyright © Belle Wallace 2000, used with permission (www.tascwheel.com)

to build such reflections into as many lessons as possible. The box shows how this might be achieved in practice.

★ *Logovisual thinking*

Logovisual thinking (LVT for short) is a tool and methodology to improve learning in classrooms. The equipment needed is as simple as a set of post-it notes and some flipchart paper, though more robust versions are available that are reusable and will last years.

Logovisual thinking encourages learners to share their ideas by recording them on moveable objects (e.g. post-it notes). These are then organized on a display surface (e.g. flipchart paper), often in the form of a concept map. LVT usually follows five steps as follows:

- **Focus**: a stimulus question focuses students' attention on the task in hand.
- **Gather**: the ideas are recorded on post-it notes.
- **Organize**: some structure is given to the ideas, typically by clustering them together.
- **Understand**: conclusions are drawn about the ideas generated, using the higher-order thinking skill of synthesis. At this stage, the ideas are usually arranged in some form of diagram or flowchart, which shows the links between them.
- **Apply**: here the ideas generated are used to carry out some other specific task: for example, writing an essay, producing a report, preparing a presentation.

LVT has been likened to a sophisticated form of brainstorming by some people. It actually goes several steps further than brainstorming by doing something concrete and meaningful with the ideas generated, in order to create breakthroughs in thinking.

An example of a student output generated through LVT is included in Figure 3.10.

LVT has been successfully introduced into geography classrooms over the last decade, with very powerful results. Teachers report that it increases students' motivation, helps to keep them on task and allows them to develop their creativity and higher-order thinking skills. It is certainly an approach that is designed to get your students working and thinking collaboratively.

I have made a special study of LVT over the past ten years, and the key reference source to learn more about the approach is *Making Meaning: learning through logovisual thinking* by myself,

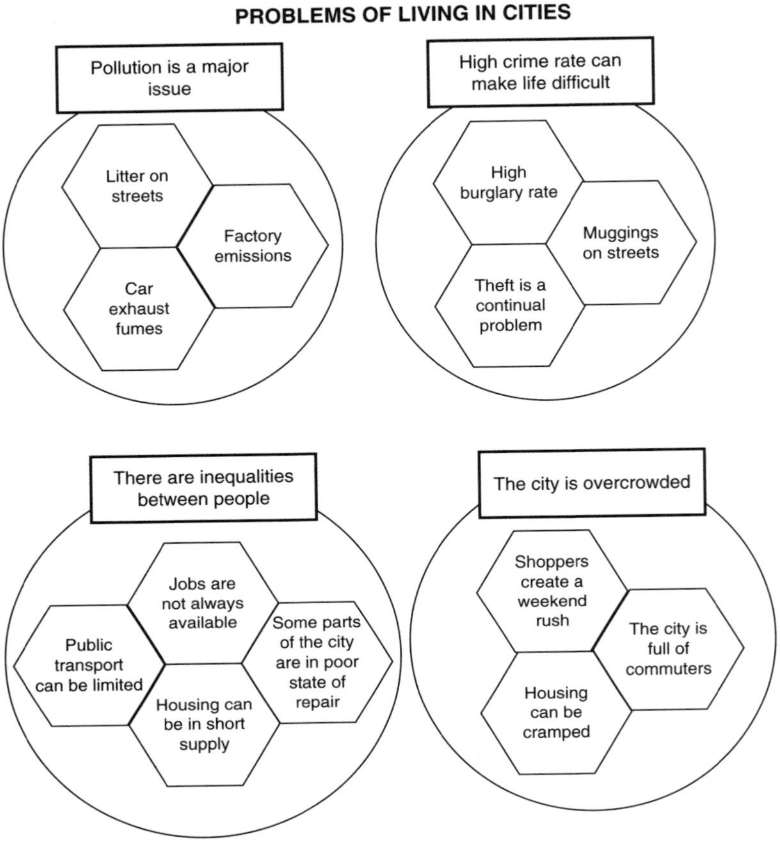

Figure 3.10 LVT lesson example (Note that in this example the students have carried out the stages Focus, Gather and Organize. The stages of Understand and Apply will follow later on.)

John Varney and Anthony Blake (Cambridge: Chris Kington Publishing, 2005). It contains worked examples of how LVT has been used to add value to classrooms across the country. You can order robust equipment (dry wipe magnetic shapes of a variety of shapes and sizes and dry wipe boards to display them on) from the Centre for Management Creativity – see www.logovisual.com for more details and lots of additional information about LVT, including many free articles and case studies.

★ *Mind maps*

Mind mapping is a way of representing and organizing thoughts in a radiant manner which fits with the way in which memory and learning are constructed. Mind maps have been around for centuries; indeed Leonardo da Vinci was using a form of mind mapping in the sixteenth century.

You should find every opportunity to enable your students to draw mind maps. Bear in mind the following about mind maps as you do so:

- Mind mapping develops from radiant thinking. This is an associative process of developing ideas and connecting them. Mind maps provide a way of visually recording and organizing ideas which relate to each other.
- Mind maps are especially useful for students who are intuitive thinkers or who favour visual methods of learning (see page 31).
- Mind maps bring with them many benefits:
  - They promote creative thinking
  - They help communicate complicated ideas
  - They aid your memory
  - They organize your thinking
  - They help you make new associations between ideas
  - They can help you learn more quickly and efficiently
- The excellent software programme Inspiration allows students to prepare electronic mind maps – see www.inspiration.com for details.

An example of a mind map is shown in Figure 3.11.

Drawing mind maps

Follow the five steps to draw a mind map:

1. Start with a key word that represents the topic you are thinking about. Place this in the centre of a blank sheet of paper, and add an image that associates with this word.
2. Draw lines radiating out from this central image, and write words along the lines that you associate with the central idea. Add images alongside these words, and use colour to make them stand out and be memorable.
3. If you come to a halt, add several blank lines and leave them, to be completed later.
4. Take each idea which you developed from the central theme and add further lines to them, writing words along the lines that you associate with these ideas. You are now building a second level of association.
5. Continue the process until your mind map is completed, then look for patterns and connections between ideas, perhaps adding links between several ideas in the map.

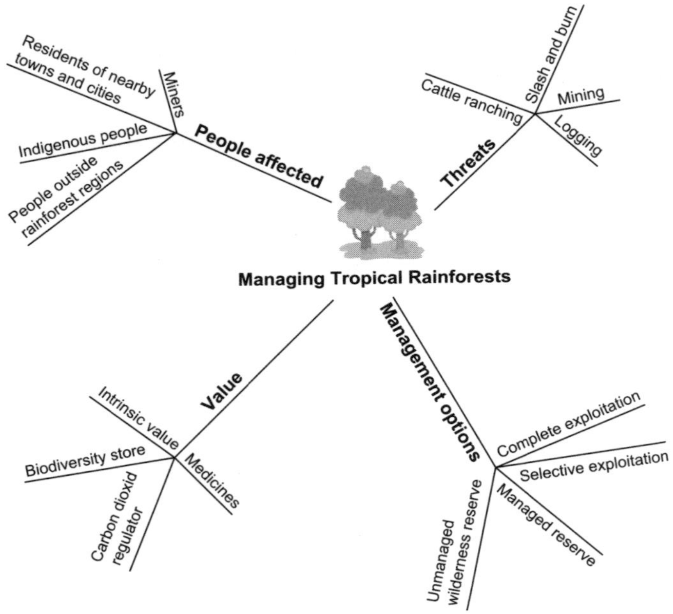

Figure 3.11 Example mind map: Managing tropical rainforests

★ *Dilemma-based learning*

Dilemma-based learning is concerned with the exploration of problems that society has to face, and is especially suited to geographical learning. Dilemma-based learning is about carrying out an enquiry about what it means to make a wise choice. It requires learners to consider their thinking and make appropriate choices. Some of main features of dilemma-based learning are as follows:

- Dilemma-based learning encourages students to engage in a specific form of enquiry (see more about enquiry-based learning on page 76).
- The main value of dilemma-based learning lies not in the acquisition of content knowledge, but in the development of learning to learn skills which are acquired en route to the resolution of the dilemma.
- It can be carried out alone or in small pairs, but is most suitable for small group work.
- It works best in classrooms where students are used to collaborative learning and groupwork – otherwise the approach needs to be introduced gradually, in adult-facilitated groups.

- It can be helpful to assign roles to the group members to ensure greater engagement in the exercise and to promote on-task behaviour, for example, by having a time keeper and a group facilitator (who keeps track of how the group is working together).
- Over time, groups will be able to become more autonomous, and the need for roles will be less of a necessity.
- It helps students to carry out higher-level thinking skills, such as the skills of creative thinking and decision-making.
- There is often no clear-cut solution to dilemmas – indeed some of the most effective thinking in considering dilemmas comes from close consideration of various alternative solutions.
- Different groups should not be expected to come up with the same conclusions, but should be prepared to justify their conclusions.
- It works best when carried out towards the end of a unit of work, so that students have some detailed knowledge of the subject matter being considered.
- It has close links to thinking skills, as in order to come up with appropriate decisions on how the dilemma should be solved, it is necessary to engage in a range of different types of thinking.

A worked example of dilemma-based learning is included in the box to show how it may be incorporated into a lesson.

Dilemma-based learning case study

The following example shows how dilemma-based learning was conducted in a geography classroom.

Should a new bypass be built around our town? The focus for the dilemma was to consider whether a new bypass should be built around a rural market town. As with any such development, the new road would bring with it advantages as well as disadvantages to the rural community they are intended to serve, and for visitors.

Introduction – the topic for the dilemma-based learning activity was introduced to the class via a PowerPoint presentation, showing the location of the new road superimposed on photographs of the site. Additional details were given to explain the perceived need for the road. A whole class discussion took place, with notes being recorded on the whiteboard summarizing the pros and cons of the development.

Groupwork – the class split into groups of four to six students to work on the dilemma. The group members each had a specific role to carry out in their group. They were given 20 minutes to discuss the dilemma and come up with a decision they were comfortable with. To help them come to a decision, the students were asked to consider the road development from the point of view of a local resident overlooking the site, a resident who did not overlook the site and a visitor to the area. The range of possible solutions included the building of a two-lane road, a single carriageway road or no road at all.

Sharing the outcomes – each group then shared with the rest of the class their decision, in each case justifying it. The groups also commented on how they worked as a group and the difficulty of coming to a group decision.

Plenary – the lesson ended with the teacher leading a discussion which drew together some of the main points of the activity, in particular the range of possible solutions to the dilemma as outlined by the students. The teacher also discussed the types of thinking that each group engaged in when working on the dilemma, giving specific names to the thinking type and adding practical examples from the students' work. Finally, the teacher asked students to reflect on how well they worked in their groups. During this final part of the lesson, the activity closely resembled a metacognitive reflection (see page 83).

Homework – for homework, students were asked to write a 300-word report that summarized their group's findings. The report included a discussion of the pros and cons of their solution to the dilemma.

An excellent resource book containing very detailed advice on dilemma-based learning and its use in the classroom is *Dilemma-based Learning in the Humanities: Integrating Social, Emotional and Thinking Skills* by Phil Wood, Barry Hymer and Deborah Michel (Cambridge: Chris Kington Publishing, 2007). It contains many worked examples and makes extensive links to thinking skills, philosophy for children and other aspects of learning. Task 3.13 challenges you to come up with some dilemmas of your own.

Task 3.13: Dilemma-based learning in your classroom

Study the text on dilemma-based learning. Use your creative thinking skills to come up with the titles of five dilemma-based learning activities for a specific year group. What are the intended learning outcomes of these dilemmas, and what resources will you need for each? Select one and carry out the activity, review its success, then try another, this time getting a colleague to observe your lessons and provide feedback on strengths and weaknesses of the dilemma-based learning activity.

★ *Effective questioning techniques*

One of the most important classroom techniques to master is the use of effective questioning in order to extend students' thinking and create effective learning experiences. Questioning comes in many forms and can be used to clarify students' understanding, prompt further thinking and help students to build new knowledge into existing frameworks. Bear in mind the following about questioning:

- Both open and closed questions have value, but students' thinking is best extended where open questions are used. Closed questions are those that can be answered with 'yes' or 'no' responses.
- It is important to vary the questions you ask your students, blending open and closed questions and a range of different question prompts (see box).
- There are key links between questioning style and thinking skills in that questions can lead learners through different levels of thinking in Bloom's taxonomy, including higher-order thinking.
- Higher-order questioning is a way of helping your students to carry out higher-order thinking (see box).
- Get students to come up their own effective geographical questions as well as posing them yourself. Encourage them to work together in pairs and groups in order to ask each other insightful questions.
- Give students plenty of 'wait time' before seeking a response – at least 20 seconds – this gives them time to come up with an appropriate response rather than just saying the first thing that comes into their heads.
- Include some 'no hands up' periods during your questioning sessions – instead, pick on students randomly in order to elicit a response. This ensures that more reflective thinking is carried out, and all students get an equal chance of being picked.
- Self-questioning is a very valuable tool in solving geographical problems – help learners to devise suitable questions to ask themselves (see box).
- Students can ask and answer questions on sticky notes – providing an alternative to conventional methods of questioning. Some students may prefer the anonymity that accompanies this kind of approach to questioning.

Fun and challenge can be injected into the classroom by staging a question time event or a panel show where the audience asks questions that are answered by the panel.

Question prompts

The following question prompts can be used in your classroom:

- *What? Who? When? Why?* – particularly effective when analysing a photograph.
- *To what extent?* – helps students to evaluate the degree to which something occurs. It is an example of a higher-order question.
- *What would X think about this?* – gets students thinking about a particular person's view on a subject.
- *What if?* – helps students to think about future scenarios and speculate on possible outcomes.
- *What can geographers do to help people understand this?* – gets students to think about the role of geographers in helping to make sense of the world. This is another example of a higher-order question.
- *Evaluate the success of . . .* – challenges students to make judgements about whether something meets its aims. Another example of a higher-level question.

Self-questioning prompts

Here are just a few examples of self-questioning prompts which can be used to help students to get out of a rut when stuck:

- Why am I doing things this way?
- What assumptions am I making?
- Is this the best way to do this?
- How can I change the way I'm thinking about this?
- In what other ways could I do this?

Task 3.14: Investigating your questioning style

Study the above text on questioning. What kinds of questioning techniques do you currently use in your classroom? How effective are they at developing higher-order thinking? What new questioning strategies could you try out in future?

★ *Cross-curricular links*

Throughout this book I have tried to make links between geography and other areas of the curriculum. Some schools have exploited these links by staging cross-curricular days or weeks where students have studied one topic from the point of view of a range of subject disciplines. Others have simply mapped the links and encouraged students to see how their learning dovetails with other areas of the curriculum. Whatever approach you take, it is important to be aware of the many links that exist between geography and other areas of the curriculum and to make your students aware of these too. Other points to bear in mind about cross-curricular links are as follows:

- Geography is perhaps unique in its ability to encompass a holistic view of some of the challenges facing society today – there are few, if any, school subjects that are not touched upon during the study of a geography course.
- They encourage your students to see geography as just one part of a much wider web of knowledge that exists in the real world outside the school gates.
- In secondary schools, we tend to compartmentalize subjects far too readily, with students not seeing the links between the different subjects they study. It is not uncommon for a student to claim to be good at one subject, but no good at another, that in reality has many similarities in terms of what is required of the students.
- Students can be helped to engage with the subject of geography if they see its relevance to the other subjects they study, for example, through the links between mathematics and the mechanics of erosion, or English and the need for effective communication in geography.
- A sound understanding of subjects such as science can aid the development of geographical knowledge and understanding, for example, the structure of the atmosphere or the process of soil formation.
- Making links to other aspects of the curriculum can provide some exciting opportunities for fun and highly engaging geography lessons, for example, the study of African tribal dances as a way of communicating information about climatic conditions and how these affect plant growth. Bringing these subjects into the geography classroom can help to engage students who may not find geography an intrinsically interesting subject (yes, strangely enough there *are* students who don't like geography!).
- Making links with other areas of the syllabus also encourages students to develop transferable skills, something which should be a key target for any teacher. Too often, students fail to be able to transfer what they can do in one subject to another.

Task 3.15: Your cross-curricular links

Think about the cross-curricular links you make in your teaching of a specific year group. Draw a mind map (see page 86) that illustrates these cross-curricular links. Then assess the balance in terms of the subjects you link to. Which subjects do you make most links to? Which subject has few links? Add in a different colour ways in which you could make additional links to subject areas which are not currently well covered. You could repeat the exercise for another year group if you wish to expand the cross-curricular links you are making.

★ *Enriching the geography curriculum*

There are many ways in which to enrich the geography curriculum, and this section takes a look at some of the principal methods that can be employed in your school. Enrichment is about additionality; adding something new to the subject of geography in a way that makes it more interesting, engaging or worthy of study. Consider the following when planning your enrichment activities:

- Enrichment is concerned with extending the geography curriculum, taking things beyond the normal boundaries of the subject into new and exciting realms.
- Enrichment can take place within geography lessons and can also form part of extra-curricular activities such as clubs.
- Enrichment is designed to enhance the regular curriculum, adding something fresh to what is normally taught in a way that complements the standard curriculum.
- Enrichment aims to help students gain a more rounded grasp of geography as a subject, as well as gain valuable additional skills.
- Well-organized enrichment can also have benefits in terms of passing examinations, with the inclusion of much relevant syllabus content.
- Enrichment can take advantage of subject areas outside geography in order to bring a new dimension to the study of the subject.

Examples of geography enrichment activities include the following:

- Guest speakers.
- An environment club, which carries out practical conservation activities on the school grounds and in the local community.

- An orienteering, hiking or fell-running club (all require map-reading skills and get students outdoors where many landforms and other physical features of the landscape can be seen).
- A geography magazine team which produces a regular publication with geography-related stories.
- A geography web team which takes responsibility for a special student section of the geography VLE content.
- A University Challenge-style interform geography quiz with a special prize for the winning team.
- Visits to places of geographical interest outside of school.
- The production of geographically themed artwork.
- The delivery of an assembly to peers on a geographical subject.
- The production of short stories for younger pupils which include some geographical content (see also page 99).

Task 3.16: Enrichment explored

Study the text on enrichment. Draw up a list of the enrichment methods you currently use in your classroom. What additional methods mentioned in the text do you think would be worthwhile? Identify three, and prepare a plan for how they will be introduced into lessons. If there are resource implications, check out the funding sources in Chapter 5.

★ *Celebrating and promoting geography*

The best geography departments actively promote the subject and students successes within and beyond their schools. They find every opportunity to fly the flag for geography and draw people's attention to its many positive features. There are plenty of ways in which you can celebrate and promote geography, including:

- Writing articles or getting students to write articles about geography in the school magazine/newsletter.
- Having prominent display boards in public areas as well as in the department.
- Staging assemblies on a geographical theme.
- Holding an annual 'geography day' where everybody is encouraged to think about a burning geographical issue.
- Issuing regular press releases to newspapers about work in the geography department – there is nothing more powerful for parents than seeing your department featured in the newspaper.

- Having a geography in the news noticeboard where topical articles are posted to show the links between geographical studies and the real world.
- Submitting articles to professional journals about the work of your department (e.g. *Teaching Geography*).
- Applying for quality marks and awards for innovative work – this can bring in much-needed funds too.

All these kinds of departmental 'marketing' will benefit from the setting up of a student publicity team, made up of talented students who help to fly the flag for the subject. In any department which is well led, there are likely to be several especially keen students who are happy to fulfil this role. There are many rewards for the participating students, including seeing their work in print, as well as the fact that their geography knowledge, understanding and skills are being developed. In order to be able to explain geography to an outside audience, students first have to understand it comprehensively themselves.

Some of the most effective publicity work stresses the links between geography and the daily lives of all of us, illustrating the many ways in which geography shapes our lives. Do not assume that students and the wider community will recognize these kinds of links; they sometimes need to be spelled out in order to be understood.

★ *Action research*

Geography presents some wonderful opportunities for so-called action research, namely, research carried out by teachers into geography as a subject and what is effective in the classroom in engaging young geographers' minds. The way action research is organized will be familiar to geography teachers as it mirrors the enquiry-based approach to learning that is one of the principal hallmarks of the subject.

Six steps to action research:

- *Identify a suitable research question to investigate* – make this as specific as possible.
- *Gather data* – this can be in a range of formats including test results, lesson observation, questionnaires and student interviews.
- *Present the data* – using graphs, charts or other diagrams.
- *Analyse the data* – this can be done simply or using statistical packages.
- *Draw conclusions* – drawing together all the strands and summing up the key findings.

- *Evaluate the research* – consider the strengths and weaknesses, and present recommendations for how things could be improved next time.

There are very many action research titles that can be investigated in your geography classroom. To give a flavour of what is possible, here are five questions to consider – Task 3.17 asks you to think about action research in your classroom:

- What contribution do websites make to the study of geography at key stage 3?
- What makes geography a popular option subject at GCSE?
- How can mapwork be improved through the use of ICT?
- How can fieldwork at key stage 4 help students make geographical sense of their local area?
- How can student voice at key stage 5 be used to enhance the teaching of geography?

Task 3.17: Action research in your classroom

Think about some of the burning issues or priorities for the next half-term in terms of classroom practice. Come up with three possible action research questions that will help you to make your lessons even more effective. Discuss these with another member of your department to identify the topic that is most suitable for your action research. Carry out the action research, and present the results to other staff as part of a staff meeting. The best schools routinely include such staff professional development activities in their staff meetings. Make sure your presentation includes recommendations for how, benefitting from the action research, your lessons (and perhaps those of others) can be improved.

In order to share the results of your research, you should consider writing it up for one of the professional journals for geographers, such as the GA's *Teaching Geography*. This will allow the widest range of fellow geography teachers to benefit from the research you have done, as well as being an excellent addition to your personal portfolio for appraisal purposes.

Action research can also provide the springboard for some more in-depth research, which may form part of a Master's or Doctoral study. There are also possibilities to team up with a university to carry out a collaborative project. There are many exciting avenues to pursue that will add a new dimension to your teaching and the learning of your students. Some very significant findings have come from teachers' research carried out in their own classrooms. Carrying out research will also make you a more reflective teacher.

★ *Innovative approaches*

The teaching of geography can be enlivened through the use of a range of innovative approaches which add an extra dimension to the study of the subject, or cast fresh light on familiar classroom challenges. A wide range of examples are discussed below to show the kind of thing that is possible.

Guest speakers

The subject of geography can be brought to life by inviting guest speakers to come to your school to speak about their experiences of geography and how the subject affects their lives. Some examples include:

- *Businesspeople* – especially the links to economic geography and industrial processes.
- *Farmers* – especially the links to weather and climate and farming.
- *University lecturers* – presenting details of their specialist fields of interest.
- *Newspaper editors and journalists* – discussing details of geography-related stories in the press.
- *Mountaineers/climbers* – especially the links to landforms and map-reading skills.
- *Scientists* – if briefed properly, these people can help to demystify some of the key issues in geography.
- *Local council staff* – explaining some of the local issues affecting the community.
- *Advocates of fair trade* – explaining the background to the issues.
- *Representatives of charities* – such as Oxfam, the Soil Association or Friends of the Earth, explaining to students the nature of their work.

It is important to brief all guest speakers who visit your school to maximize the benefits of their visits. They should be given details of year groups/age ranges, encouraged to have a clear focus for their talks and advised to keep their session as interactive as possible. The last thing you want is to have them talking at your students for the whole lesson, with few chances for them to engage with the speaker. Make sure you make the most of the visit by getting a student to write it up for the school newsletter/

magazine (ensuring a copy is sent to the speaker), and get another to write a thank you letter on behalf of the class. It is vital to nurture your guest speakers if they are to return. Continued positive links with the local community rely on managing the relationship in these ways.

Having guest speakers is an excellent way to enthuse students who may not normally find the subject interesting, as the students sometimes see a relevance of the subject that they had not realized before. Bringing in people who are well known locally, such as a high-profile mountaineer, adds great credentials to your department and can inspire students. The benefits of having a guest speaker who is 'cool' to students cannot be overstated and can give your department a significant boost.

Good news for geography students

A geography department in a North Yorkshire school managed to secure the sponsorship of *The Independent* in order to provide a complimentary daily copy of the newspaper in order to help students to gain an appreciation of current affairs linked to the subject of geography. Students scanned through and cut out copies of geography-related stories which were kept in a special filing area which was accessible to staff and students. These were used by teachers to bring to life the teaching of certain topics, as well as being scrutinized by students who were researching topics as part of individual projects and coursework. A display board was also installed with articles displayed which were relevant to the topics currently being studied by the different year groups. The provision of the newspaper was successful in improving students' awareness of current affairs linked to the geography syllabus. You too could benefit from such an arrangement by seeking the support of a local, regional or national newspaper.

Creative writing

There are some excellent ways to use creative writing to enliven the subject of geography. One example is the writing of short stories for younger children which convey geographical content. For example, students in year 10 could prepare a story for year 6 pupils called 'Walter the water droplet' which explains the water cycle through the use of Walter's journey from the ocean to the sky and through rivers back to the ocean again. There are many other possibilities of such short stories, and handing over the choice of subject matter to the students can result in some very creative outcomes. Poems with a geographical theme are also a great way to use creative writing to brighten up the subject. For example, students could write a poem expressing the views and emotions of somebody whose home has been destroyed by a hurricane.

Debates and role plays

The subject of geography lends itself to some wonderful interactive teaching through debates and role plays. Such learning approaches work especially well in geography because of the many sides to some of the key issues which are studied in the subject. Some examples of debates and role plays that in the author's experience have worked especially well include:

- A decision on a major local development: for example, wind farm, supermarket, bypass.
- The development of the rainforest in a specific country, with different groups representing various interested parties.
- A public enquiry into whether a new housing estate should be built on the outskirts of town.

By staging debates, you will be helping to improve students' oracy skills (providing a link to the English department) as well as their geographical knowledge and skills.

Geographical assemblies

Why not raise awareness of your subject by staging regular geographical assemblies? These can also provide an excellent focus for student work, and students can take part in the presentation of the assembly. Some ideal topics for geographical assemblies include the following:

- Local issues which require a decision or are controversial in some way (e.g. a new supermarket or road-building scheme).
- International issues of interest to young people (e.g. the destruction of the rainforests, global warming and sea level rise).
- Geographical issues that have direct relevance to the lives of young people.
- Topics which require the student audience to vote.
- Topics which allow some interaction between the presenters and the audience.

When presenting geographical assemblies, try to hand over the ownership to students wherever possible to allow them to develop their presentational skills. Such assemblies are also excellent ways to educate the audience on certain geographical issues, with the added benefit of their peers taking the lead in doing the educating.

Geography newsletter

You could issue a periodic geography newsletter to draw attention to important geographical issues which have local relevance. Such a newsletter will also provide the opportunity for students to write for a purpose on a geographical theme. Some ideal topics for a newsletter could include:

- River flooding
- Unusual weather events
- The occurrence of natural hazards
- Progress on new building projects locally
- Tourism visitor patterns to key attractions.

You can make the production of your geography newsletter quite sophisticated by creating specific roles for the students on the team. For example, editor, news editor, features editor, picture editor etc. This has the added benefit of helping to develop journalistic skills (e.g. crafting articles, meeting deadlines etc.) and creating a sense of responsibility among the production team.

Writing geography booklets

Students can gain much by being challenged to write mini geography books on a range of topics, aimed at their peers or a younger audience. The preparation of such booklets requires students to assimilate information and present it in an easily understood format for another audience. Booklets can be illustrated with visual material taken from the internet or prepared by the students. One approach that has worked well has been for year 7 students to prepare introductory booklets for children in year 6, which introduce them to some of the major topics in geography. Geography booklets are an ideal way of developing students' skills in writing for a specific audience, which has the added benefit of having clear links to the English syllabus.

Lucky dip

Fun can be injected into the geography classroom by challenging students, working in groups, to present the results of their work on a geography topic in a range of ways. The names of various presentation methods are written on pieces of card, which are then placed in a box. A student represent from each group picks a card from the box, and the students have two lessons to research the topic and deliver the results using the required presentation method. A variation on lucky dip is to give students a range of suggestions and get them to pick their favourite presentation method from the list. Suitable methods of presentation can be very varied and can include:

- PowerPoint presentation
- Role play
- Rap/song/poem
- Poster
- News/radio broadcast
- Animation.

The conclusion of this work is to have each group present their work to the rest of the class, during a 'show and tell' lesson. The audience is required to make notes in the form of a mind map or other graphic organizer, summarizing the key points of each presentation.

Geography dictionary

Students can build their vocabulary by preparing their own geography dictionary during the course of their GCSE or A-level studies. Every student should be issued with a small (A5 or A6) size notebook at the start of the school year, and every time a new geography keyword is encountered, this should be recorded with its definition, A–Z style. Such notebooks can become invaluable during revision for end-of-unit tests and examinations. The notebooks can be made more visually appealing by the student adding an illustration beneath each keyword.

Geography blockbusters

You can have a great deal of fun while also developing students' geographical knowledge by playing Geography Blockbusters. This is best done through a data projector by projecting a pre-prepared Blockbuster grid onto the wall. Students then work their way across the grid by correctly identifying the geographical word which is signified by each letter. The letters change to a solid hexagon when the correct answer is found. Blockbusters is an ideal game to play as a plenary to recap some of the geographical words covered during the lesson, or at the end of unit of study to summarize the key content. You can download some free software for creating blockbuster grids at www.prometheanplanet.com.

End-of-topic quiz

When you reach the end of a topic, you can breathe fresh life into the familiar end-of-unit test by instead staging a quiz in which the class is split into two groups, and the students set the questions for each other. Desks can be arranged opposite each other to bring a sense of occasion to the quiz, and you as teacher can act as quiz master, posing the questions to each side in turn and filtering out any especially difficult or otherwise inappropriate questions. Questions of various types can be set, including:

- True or false – for example, the centre of a town is called the Central Business District, true or false?
- Spot the odd one out – for example, spot the odd city out from the following list: London, Paris, New York, Moscow, Rio de Janeiro (answer: Rio de Janeiro because it's in an economically developing country).
- Define this word – for example, define the word corrosion.
- Bigger or smaller, higher or lower – for example, which river is longer: the Nile or the Amazon?

Any questions?

The teacher sits in the centre of the room with the students all around. The teacher thinks of a geographical word and to determine what the word is, the students ask relevant questions which only require a yes or no answer. The class could be split up into teams to bring a competitive edge to this exercise. A variation on this theme (suitable for teachers who are not stage shy) is for the teacher to come dressed as a famous figure in geography (an explorer or well-known scientist, for example). Again, questions with a yes or no answer are asked, this time to determine the identity of the teacher.

Kinaesthetic learning in action

Much has been written about the importance of providing learning opportunities which respect students' learning preferences (see page 31 for general guidance on this topic). Kinaesthetic learning opportunities allow students to get physically involved in their learning, using their bodies to engage with the subject matter.

An example of an innovative way to do this in lessons comes from the study of food webs, which forms an important part of any discussion of the management of any habitats such as tropical rainforests. It requires a certain amount of 'buy in' by students, but has been shown to work effectively with students of all ages.

The task involves students physically acting out how organisms are arranged in a forest food web. This requires the use of a large amount of floor space, so the tables and chairs should all be cleared to the edge of the room for this exercise (this can be done by the students in the class prior to the food web lesson to save time). Begin by asking a group of students to act out the role of the primary producers (trees and plants). To do this, they sit on the floor in a line and pretend to be living trees or plants, perhaps swaying in the wind. Next, a small group of students (smaller than the primary producers) acts out the role of primary consumers; these are the organisms that eat the primary producers. Each student should act out the role of a specific primary consumer, which will be different according to the food web being studied. The students can pretend to be eating the primary producers, mimicking the true feeding relationships in the food web. Inevitably this part of the lesson generates humour as the trees and plants are 'eaten' by such things as caterpillars, bugs and slugs. Next, a smaller group of students acts out the role of secondary consumers, with such things as birds and mammals 'eating' the primary consumers. The final stage involves the introduction of a tertiary consumer, a top predator such as a big cat or eagle that 'eats' the secondary consumers. To complete the exercise, all the living things are asked to join hands with an organism which eats them, making a living representation of the food web. This exercise, as well as being fun, has been shown to be highly memorable and easily recalled when knowledge of food webs is required in examinations.

The food web example is just one way in which kinaesthetic learning can be used in the classroom. Other examples are as follows:

- The creation of living bar charts as students display information about a topic by creating a graphic representation using their own bodies.
- The use of hand gestures to simulate the three types of plate margins as follows: constructive – wrists together, palms facing away from each other; conservative – flat hands rubbing against each other in opposite

directions; destructive – the fingers of one hand going beneath the knuckles of the other.

- A puppet show – students can make finger puppets and act out a scenario to demonstrate geographical knowledge, for example, the effects of earthquakes. This provides a creative outlet for those of your students which enjoy performance.
- Learning through dance – adventurous teachers can explore how dance can add value to geography lessons in a number of ways. For example, samba dancing can be practised when studies of the Brazilian rainforest are made, or a Masai (Kenyan) jumping dance can be used when studies of African rural communities are carried out.

These methods are very useful in engaging students who may not instinctively find the study of geography very interesting, as they allow students to express themselves in unconventional ways in the geography classroom. I have seen the dramatic effects they can have on students with a creative streak, whose creativity is released by these methods, and whose opinion of geography as a subject has changed as a result of the kinaesthetic learning methods.

Methods of kinaesthetic learning can present ideal opportunities for cross-curricular working, for example, with the art, music or dance departments. Such cross-curricular working is rare but is an excellent way of combining the skills of different subject teachers, as well as helping students to see beyond the imposed boundaries of the secondary school curriculum.

Kinaesthetic learning represents, of course, just one way of appealing to the learning preferences of students. For more classroom guidance about how you can cater for different learning preferences, see page 32.

Keeping it current

Geography is a living, breathing subject, and it is important to take every opportunity to remind students of the topicality of the subject. One way this can be done is to ask students, in turn, to bring in an interesting news clipping on a current geographical issue that has local, national or international interest: for example, flood, famine, new development etc. Prepare a wall display by theme, and get students to stick their news clipping on the relevant theme, and then spend a few minutes explaining the main points of the news clipping to the rest of the class, as well as outlining their own views on it. This helps to keep geography fresh and relevant to the lives of the students. It will also help students to think of geography as a subject that is highly relevant today, and which they need to have an opinion on.

Using unusual stimuli

Geography is a subject that lends itself to the use of unusual stimuli for lessons. One approach that I took with my A-level group was to look at household items and think about how I could turn them into innovative lesson ideas. One of the best activities I came up with began when I opened a packet of bagels. The packet for the brand of bagels I had bought had the phrase 'the authentic New York taste' written on its side. As we were studying urban geography at the time, I hit upon the idea of using this as a stimulus to investigate the pros and cons of living in New York in order to discover what the 'authentic New York taste' might be like. I took the bagels into school and explained my thinking to my students. The task set was for the students to research quality of life in New York in order to investigate the advantages and disadvantages of living in the city. They were given two lessons to carry out the research, at the end of which they had to come to some conclusions as to what the authentic New York taste was like, and whether on the whole the city was a good or bad place in which to live. The students were given a range of stimulus materials, including articles from *National Geographic* and newspapers, and were also given access to the internet. They were also given recording sheets on which to systematically record their ideas. The conclusion they came up with was that it depended who you were: New York could be both a good and a bad place in which to live, depending on your socio-economic status. In this way, the authentic New York taste was seen to vary from person to person. The lesson was completed by the students eating the bagels to discover what the authentic New York bagel taste was like! This learning activity demonstrates that innovation can be found in many forms, and even the most unlikely stimulus can sometimes be turned into lesson ideas. The message here is that when looking for inspiration for your lessons, do not overlook the many potential stimuli that surround you in the form of everyday objects.

Letting students take the lead at student review meetings

You can bring a whole new dimension to key stage 4 and 5 student review meetings by handing over more responsibility to students in a way that is sure to impress parents. This can be done by asking the students to comment on their strengths, weaknesses and marks over the course of the term. The lesson before the review meeting can be used to prepare for it by looking over their student record card (see page 56) and noting down key points to be made in the review meeting, with the help of a crib sheet (see below). Any students struggling to do this can be helped via a one-to-one session with the teacher. Each student also records the things they need to do to improve their performance in geography, what the teacher can specifically help them with and an indication of their target grade. During the review evening, the student comments on their performance as described above, followed by additional comments by the teacher, perhaps also illustrated with examples of students' work. Parents are then invited to ask questions or make comments of their own. Some students may also wish to identify things that their parents can do to help them to achieve their target grade in geography. This helps to emphasize the sense of partnership between student, teacher and parents.

My own experience of running student review evenings of this nature is that they prove much more engaging for students, and that given the responsibility, they are more than capable, with the help of their record card, of identifying their strengths and weaknesses in the subject, and what they need to do to reach their target grade. Furthermore, there is often a striking similarity between the areas for improvement identified by the student and those identified by the teacher. The challenge for the teacher is to note carefully what they need to do to help each student to reach their target grade, and then to try their utmost to do these things.

The act of handing over responsibility to students in this way is very empowering for young people, and its value in motivating them should not be underestimated. It provides a wonderful opportunity to show students that they are responsible for their own learning and can identify things they need to do to improve their performance.

Student review evening crib sheet

- What marks have you gained for the recent geography assignments?
- What have you enjoyed over the last term?
- What are your strengths and weaknesses in geography?
- What do you plan to work on to improve your performance in this subject?
- How can your teacher help you to achieve this?
- What is your target grade in geography?

Funding your innovative geography work

If you are wondering how you might find the funds to carry out innovative ideas that have resource implications, the good news is that there are many sources of external funding which can be used to add a creative element to your geography work. Few geography teachers realize that there are actually hundreds of millions of pounds in external funds available each year to support innovative teaching in schools. Many of the funding sources lend themselves especially well to geography teaching and geography-related extra-curricular activities.

The following examples show how geography teachers have used external funds to enrich their lessons. Additionally, several of the case studies were funded using such external funding sources, and a list of further funding sources are given in Section 6. Note the appearance of several entries for Settle High School reflects the author's time as head of geography at the school.

Settle millennium map

A head of geography was successful in gaining £600 for his rural comprehensive school in order to produce a map of the town at the turn of the millennium. Funding came from the Frederick Soddy Trust (see page 161). The map was researched and produced by students in year 9 as part of their geography lessons. The work was linked to an extended period of fieldwork in the local community which investigated visitor patterns, shopping activities and the sphere of influence of the town. The project successfully raised the profile of the subject among students, leading to greater enthusiasm for it in year 10. One student commented, after completing the work: 'I've learnt more about Settle in the last year than I have in the rest of my life!' This activity could easily be replicated for all or part of your local settlement.

Settle environment fair

A grant of £10,000 was secured from the charity Human Scale Education (see page 161) to stage a large-scale event which brought over 1,000 primary school children to their local secondary school for a day of environment-themed activities. The activities were led by the students at the secondary school and their teachers. The event also provided the chance for the primary school children to present the results of their own environmental projects, which had been carried out in the weeks prior to the environment fair. The event was a huge success, bringing learning alive for the primary school children and helping the secondary school students to develop their geographical knowledge and leadership skills. Some secondary school students who had not traditionally been very engaged with their learning gained much from this event, rising ably to the challenge of working with the primary school children. The event brought great credit to the secondary school and raised the profile of geography for the primary school pupils and their parents.

Yorkshire dales award

Settle High School geography department won a prize of £350 for its work to promote students' knowledge of the Yorkshire Dales National Park. The prize was awarded in recognition of the various ways in which the department had used the park as a tool for learning. This included the inclusion of a special coursework unit on tourism effects in the Dales. This award shows that making innovative changes to the curriculum can reap impressive financial rewards. Note also that no extra work as such was required to be eligible for this award; instead a change of *emphasis* was needed in the teaching schemes that underpinned the lessons. You can check out any similar schemes being organized in the national parks nearest to your school by contacting their education officers. More details of all the United Kingdom's national parks can be found at www.nationalparks.gov.uk.

A-level coursework prizes

The Settle High School geography department gained two prizes simply by entering its A-level students' work into competitions. The first, worth £350, was awarded in the form of the Chartered Institute of Logistics and Transport School Travel Prize (for details of this organization, see www.ciltuk.org.uk), for a student's study of traffic patterns and the need for a bypass in her home village. The second, much more substantial, prize of £2,000 came from the Willmot Pertwee School Competition for a study of river quality along the river Ribble. These examples show that funds can sometimes be gained just by entering coursework, without any need to carry out additional work. There are parallel schemes to the ones mentioned here aimed at GCSE and key stage 3 students, so it always pays to read carefully any fliers than arrive in your in-tray with details of such competitions. The *Times Educational Supplement* also lists details of many award schemes for schools and should be scanned on a regular basis.

Junk sculpture

Oldfield School in Bath won £500 from the School Innovation Awards (now ceased, but Awards for All cover similar ground, see page 157) to build their own environmental sculpture on the school grounds. Working with a community artist, students from the school researched the problem of waste in their local area and then selected various materials to use in a large-scale sculpture to stand on the school grounds. The project was a collaboration between the geography art departments at the school and produced some superb outcomes, not least a permanent new sculpture for the school. By allowing the students to work across two subject disciplines, they were able to see the links between different areas of the syllabus.

Grounds for learning

Several secondary schools across the country have benefited from the advice and funding secured by the charity Learning through Landscapes (see page 162) to transform their grounds into multisensory learning environments. Although it is necessary to join this charity to gain their initial support, the expert advice available through their newsletters and consultants more than makes up for the initial financial outlay (£60 for secondary schools). Schools working in partnership with Learning through Landscapes have secured grants of up to £10,000 from a range of funders in order to make the most out of their grounds as a resource for learning. This has included developments of interest to geography teachers as well as other subject areas as follows:

- The erection of a weather recording station to stimulate interest in this aspect of the geography curriculum.

- The building of nature trails to encourage the identification of tree, plant and bird species on the school grounds.
- The building of ponds to study food webs and chains.
- The building of an outdoor amphitheatre-style classroom for open air demonstrations.

Schools that have worked with Learning through Landscapes have seen a step change in the way their grounds are used as a learning resource, which is bringing profound benefits to the students at these schools.

Africa day

A school in the midlands secured £5,000 from Awards for All to stage a spectacular Africa day, which drew attention to the challenges facing this continent today. The day began with a Ghanian dancing demonstration during assembly and quickly led into a series of lessons highlighting the contemporary challenges faced by Africa. These included feeding its people, protecting the environment and sustainable economic development. Throughout the day, students were challenged to make pledges for how they might be able to help the people of Africa; these were brought together at the end of the day on a gigantic 'pledge wall' which was filled with post-it notes detailing the actions the students would be carrying out. A feature of the day was the collaboration of a number of other subject teachers to bring the event to life, such as the music and drama teachers who helped with the Ghanian dance demonstration.

Linking communities across the globe

An internationally important project was organized by a geography teacher from Royston High School in Barnsley, which sought to link young people in England with counterparts in southern Africa. The work benefited from over £50,000 which was raised from a wide variety of sources, including local charitable trusts, local companies and fundraising events such as bag packing in a major supermarket. The work began by transforming a neglected courtyard into an inspirational micro-river system, complete with its own mini wind turbine. This led to a link with the land-locked African country of Lesotho, with which the teacher had an existing contact. A major fundraising drive was initiated to take a group of students to Lesotho to meet their counterparts and – most inspirationally of all – to build a wind turbine that would bring electricity to the village for the first time. This is an example of a project that has genuinely changed lives and has been used to enrich the curriculum at the school on many occasions. In order to access funds for this kind of project, the first port of call is the *Directory of Grant-making Trusts*, published by the Charities Aid Foundation and held by most large libraries.

Task 3.18: Innovative approaches in your classroom

The innovative approaches discussed above are intended to inspire you to try out some new strategies in your classroom. Draw up a short list of your top five favourite new strategies from all those set out above. Then plan how you will introduce each into your lessons. You can get into the spirit of creative lesson planning by brainstorming with some departmental colleagues to come up with some new strategies of your own for a specific unit of work. Give yourselves a break from the normal routine by holding your brainstorming session in a different venue (e.g. a hotel, somebody's house) to help lubricate the creative juices. As you brainstorm, keep in mind the main aim: to inspire students through innovative teaching and learning approaches. The work you do while brainstorming corresponds to step 2 of the Creativity Cycle ('Idea generation', see page 19); to move on to the third step – idea selection – you will need to choose which strategies you are going to actually use in the unit of work. The remainder of the eight steps to creativity will be required to implement and monitor the success of the strategies chosen.

★ *Collaboration with other schools*

It is important not to overlook the benefits of collaborating with other schools in your locality, or even further afield, in order to enrich geographical learning. A variety of approaches can be taken to make such collaboration successful:

- Students can take part in joint fieldwork investigating a local issue.
- Students can get involved in a competitive debate on a geographical theme.

- Students can prepare presentations on geographical topics to give to students from the partner school.
- Teachers can work collaboratively to tackle a common challenge in their schools, for example, by motivating disaffected learners.
- Joint examination revision sessions can be staged in the lead-up to exams, with teachers from both schools using a range of innovative methods to help prepare students for them.

There is even funding to support the collaboration between schools in the form of the independent-state school partnerships scheme – see www.suttontrust.com for more information.

4 Case studies

Sophie Craven

Overview

This chapter contains a range of up-to-date and relevant case studies of inspirational geography teaching from schools across the United Kingdom. Each represents a comprehensive profile of innovative and outstanding practice that can be replicated in your own classroom. The aim of this chapter is to show what is possible in geography lessons with imagination, creativity and hard work.

The use of ICT in teaching geography

★ *Aylesbury High School, Buckinghamshire*

The Royal Geographiical Society (RGS) offers five Innovative Geography Teaching Grants each year. The grants awarded are up to £800 each and fund innovative geography teaching for all geography teachers working in secondary schools. The grants enable geography teachers to develop imaginative, innovative or creative teaching materials and teaching methods. The aim is to serve both geography pupils and the wider teaching community. Among the 2009 recipients was Aylesbury High School, who developed the innovative use of video diaries.

Background

Aylesbury High School is a selective girls' grammar school that prides itself as being a 'busy, ambitious and forward-looking community'. Within this successful environment, the geography department's vision is to constantly innovate and achieve excellence. The department's achievements are marked by the high take-up of geography at key stage 4 and beyond and also by their high achievement in terms of exam results – which in 2009 were well above the school average.

Awards

The department's success has also been marked by a number of awards, including:

- Secondary Geography Quality Mark status awarded by the Geographical Association in 2007.
- Two-time winner of the Innovative Geography Teaching Grant (RGS) – in 2007 for an archaeological project run in conjunction with the history department, and again in 2009 for the video diaries.
- Becky Kitchen, head of department, was awarded Chartered Geographer (Teacher) status by the Royal Geographical Society in 2007.
- Becky Kitchen was awarded the RGS Ordnance Survey Award for Excellent Teaching in Secondary Geography, 2009.

Geography video diaries

Video diaries were initially used in the department as a means for students to record geography field trips, lessons and extra-curricular activities, but as the project grew, diaries were also used to promote geography throughout the school: as discussion tools after field trips, as evidence of good practice for both staff and students' portfolios and as methods of data presentation in enquiry and coursework. Video diaries were made by students of all abilities and in every year, as well as by teachers. In addition to providing a detailed digital record of geography at the school, the diaries also provided an insight into both students' and teachers' personal geographies.

The videos were used in geography throughout the key stages and for a variety of different topics. The activities were also transferable to other subjects. Some specific examples of video diary activities can be seen in Figure 4.1.

Enhancing the teaching and learning process

The use of video has enhanced geography for the students in a number of key ways. Importantly, it provides a different and fun way of interacting with people and landscapes, which promotes enjoyment in the subject. It is also invaluable for learning and teaching as it promotes Assessment for Learning (AFL; see also page 53). Students are able to very visually review their

Idea	Uses	Description
Moderating presentations	Year 8 UN population simulation debate.	Geography is a subject which lends itself to presentation, debate and role play, however, it is very difficult to evidence and moderate this work. Presentations can be videoed and then used for moderation and peer or self assessment.
'How to . . .' videos	Year 8 gifted and talented (G&T) pupils creating a 'How to draw a fieldsketch' video. Year 12 pupils creating 'How to investigate river cross-sections' video.	There are various skills required for geography which, once taught (usually at the start of Year 7) it is assumed that pupils will be able to apply. To reinforce the importance of skills and to create a library of pupil-explained techniques, various groups of students have created 'How to . . .' videos where they film themselves explaining a geographical skill in a step by step way.

Figure 4.1 Continued

Idea	Uses	Description
Learning rambles	Year 8 G&T pupils asking questions about their environment.	Having successfully used photos as a stimulus for pupils to ask geographical questions, I created the idea of a learning ramble which does a similar thing, but using video. Pupils walk around an environment and, as they do so, ask their own questions about it. Once back in the classroom one or more of their questions could be investigated. This worked particularly well with G&T pupils who put their own spin on the idea and videoed the same learning ramble but from two different perspectives – one videoed the ramble normally and the other videoed it with the camera pointing at the ground.
Personal geographies	Year 9 interviews about their image and experience of South Africa.	As an introduction to a unit on South Africa, pupils were asked to interview each other, addressing the following questions: What do you know about South Africa already? Do you have a positive or negative image of the country? Why do you think this is? Why should we study South Africa in Geography? At the end of the unit these questions were revisited to see how much their thinking had moved on.
Creating living graphs	Year 9 climate graphs.	With a video camera, a couple of metre rulers and a measuring tape, pupils can create living graphs. The idea is that they are given some data and have to create the graph using the metre rulers as the axis and themselves as the points. These are then joined together with the measuring tape. The graph can be videoed from above and then some of the 'points' on the graph can be interviewed to describe and explain the trend.

Figure 4.1 Continued

Idea	Uses	Description
Revision aids	Year 11, 12 and 13 creating revision aids by using video and Hot Potatoes software.	The exam classes chose elements of the syllabus that they wanted to revise, and videoed themselves talking about these topics for a minute or two. Hot potatoes software was then used to create gap fill exercises and quizzes based on the embedded video. These were then shared with the rest of the class and used for revision.
Creating video diaries of fieldtrips	Year 12 residential fieldtrip to North Devon.	Pupils were given a video camera and instructed to create video diaries of the fieldtrip. Some of their diaries were factual, some humorous and some decidedly obscure! These have now been edited together to create a promotional video to encourage the Year 11 pupils to take geography in the Sixth Form.
Virtual fieldtrips	Year 12 virtual fieldtrips of Aylesbury – embedding video into Google Earth.	Pupils visited a range of different sites in Aylesbury and produced a series of short videos with voiceovers describing what they could see. Back in the classroom this was embedded into Google Earth placemarks with statistical data from the census to create a virtual fieldtrip which investigated types of housing, ethnic groups and other socio-economic factors.

Figure 4.1 Various lesson ideas

performance or their results, and are able to explain why they achieved the results they got and then look at how they could improve. Student self-assessment and understanding how to improve is a key part of what the National Strategy on AFL terms 'day-to-day assessment'. The video diaries also link well into the key concept of place by encouraging students to analyse their own views of places and to see how they compare with others. The scope of the project is large in that it spans all year groups and abilities and allows both staff and students to evaluate how they 'do' geography.

Impact	Measure
Students gain an awareness of 'their personal geographies' and can describe and explain why these may be different	Assessed by discussion with students
Students have a deeper understanding of landscapes and issues investigated during fieldtrips and lessons	Levels of achievement from 2009 (with video diaries) will be compared with levels of achievement in 2008 (without video diaries).
Teachers are more consistent in their assessment of activities involving role-play/debate	Assessed by a portfolio of videos showing comparable levels of achievement from different students.

Figure 4.2 Impact on learning

Measuring and assessing the impact on learning

The video diary project has been embedded within a range of different schemes of work within the department, and the concept is also transferable across other subjects and other curriculum areas. The concepts are being disseminated to school staff through a 'learning lunch' so that other departments can use some of the ideas and resources. Figure 4.2 gives examples of impact on learning and how to measure it.

Lessons for others on innovation and creativity: The head of department speaks

'Our work is innovative and creative as we have different ways of approaching concepts, particularly those that might appear quite "dry" or difficult for students to grasp. We try out different techniques which others may not have done before, or done in a different context, and hone them so that they work to enhance students' geographical understanding. Good examples of this approach are the 'living graph' and learning rambles.

We have tried to link with other subjects while keeping the geography strong, for example, we describe the monsoon in India through art and poetry and students have to respond to this by creating their own artefact, image or poem which captures key features of the monsoon.

The other way in which we have taught is through the medium of cake! It's amazing how many geographical concepts can be taught in this way, from shanty towns to urban models and glaciated valleys to cross-sections of volcanoes. If the teacher insists that the cake is annotated fully with flags mounted on cocktail sticks then the learning can be really powerful.

We always try to use real life and sometimes complicated examples so that students understand that geography is relevant to their lives and that they can argue and discuss key geographical issues with adults. For example, Year 8 students carry out a UN conference where they are delegates from a country and have to research and present population issues from their country and possible solutions. They also have to write a press release **after** the conference'.

Practical steps and measures to becoming more creative and innovative

The key is to not be creative or innovative for the sake of it but to think about the learning which is taking place and to ensure that the geography is kept strong and integral. If the best way to teach about graphs for your students is for them to draw it, then this is what you should do. However, there are several practical steps which you could follow to become more innovative:

- **Take other people's ideas and adapt them to suit your own purpose.** There are lots of excellent places where you can share ideas or take inspiration: for example, the Geography Teaching Today website (www.geographyteachingtoday.org.uk) has a variety of different resources, and the Geographical Association conference is a fantastic place to share resources and to meet other like-minded geographers.
- **Involve your students.** When you are planning your scheme of work or deciding what to do for a lesson, ask the students to help you. They have the experience of a wide variety of lessons and know what works and what doesn't, and they may have creative ideas of their own. Taking this a stage further, you could give groups of students 10 minutes of the lesson to teach the rest of the class about a certain concept.
- **Don't be afraid to try new things out.** It may not work the first time or with that particular topic or concept, but if you don't try out your ideas, you will never know. At Aylesbury High School, the students enjoy taking risks, and if something doesn't work the first time, we try something else.
- **Don't work in a bubble.** The best way to get ideas is to share with other people. In most schools, money for CPD is tight, but bouncing ideas around your department is always useful. Having a PGCE student is also very valuable as they bring lots of ideas with them and

should be encouraged to try out different techniques in their teaching. If you can, then network with other geography teachers in your area, share resources by email or meeting up periodically.

- **Apply for an innovative teaching grant.** If you have an idea, apply to the RGS for funding. Aylesbury High School was given an innovative teaching grant for a specific purpose (video diaries), but once the department had the equipment, teachers came up with lots of other ideas which weren't directly linked to the original project.

Further information

Innovative Geography Teaching Grants www.rgs.org
Aylesbury High School website www.ahsonline.co.uk

CROSS-CURRICULAR LINKS

★ *The Belvedere Academy, Liverpool*

The Belvedere Academy, a mixed ability 11–19 girls' school in Liverpool, was opened in September 2007, and was the first independent school to become a non–fee-paying, non-selective, mixed-ability academy in the United Kingdom. Within the school, the geography department enjoys a good reputation. The department is well respected for the consistently high attainment of students, for promoting cross-curricular links and for leading the modern foreign languages specialism through joint curriculum work with a partner school in China.

The department's vision for geography

Our vision is to develop an interest in the world in each and every one of the girls that we teach. Through developing enquiring minds, we hope to create pupils with a great understanding of the positive contribution they can make to society, not only in Liverpool, but in the United Kingdom and beyond. All members of the geography department aim to develop positive and productive working relationships, based on mutual respect. All students are valued as individuals, while being challenged academically and working towards their personal best.

The Fair Trade Fashion Show

Belvedere Academy was awarded an £800 Royal Geographical Society Innovative Geography Teaching Grant to organize a Fair Trade Fashion Show. The fashion show, staged in June 2008, was organized and run by year 9 geography students, in conjunction with the textiles department as part of a module of work on geographical issues. The whole event, including clothes worn, music, lighting, refreshments and ticket sales was organized by students.

Inspired by their learning in geography, students were given the opportunity to present some of their own fashion garments through a cross-curricular working relationship with the textiles department. This enabled students to adapt clothes or create clothes or accessories of their own. A textiles enrichment session was run after school so that all students could attend, if they wished, to complete their work. The clothes that the models wore were either influenced by fair trade and designed by the students themselves, or donated by local companies and organizations including Marks & Spencer – Gemini, Liverpool University and Shared Earth.

Nichol Waring from Marks & Spencer, who regularly arranges fashion shows on the company's behalf, visited the school in May during an after-school enrichment session. During the session, Nichol measured models, matched colours and styles and talked to students about their roles within the fashion show. Such was the excitement around the event, even at this early stage, that other students came along to watch the fitting.

Marks & Spencer kindly donated a fair trade food and drink hamper that could be raffled at the fashion show. They also donated 'bags for life', money-off vouchers and samples of fair trade tea, coffee and chocolate for the audience.

Teaching and Learning was enhanced and brought to life by another external visitor – Sophie Shepherd, the manager of Shared Earth, Liverpool. Sophie visited the school the week before the fair trade fashion show, during an after-school geography enrichment session, to talk about her experiences of travelling to India with her employers. She was able to talk to the students about working conditions with and without fair trade, show images of her trip and pass around fair trade products and accessories. By having someone who had seen conditions in Indian factories first hand, the students were really able to get a feel for the different economic and social conditions. The unique, high-quality talk that Sophie gave opened up the issues of fair trade and fashion beyond the year 9 curriculum to an audience of over 40, from a mixture of all year groups.

The Innovative Geography Teaching Grant provided the school with an ideal opportunity to update existing schemes of work to include the study of fair trade, and also allowed them to purchase some more up-to-date resources for the fashion topic that already formed part of the geographical issues module.

The fair trade fashion show was a huge success. Students were really engaged by the real-life stories that they were presented with. Having external speakers and visitors helped to emphasize the importance of what they were learning about and that fair trade has real relevance to geography in a real-life context.

For further details of the RGS Grant scheme, see the Aylesbury High School 'Video Diaries' case study on page 116 and the funding ideas section on page 156.

Project outcomes

- One year 9 student has been requested to contact Marks & Spencer – Gemini regarding modelling in the future.
- Increased confidence of students in their organizational and presentational skills as well as increased personal confidence.
- Maintenance of high numbers of students choosing geography as a GCSE option despite increased subject choice.
- The establishment of a good working relationship between The Belvedere Academy and local fair trade suppliers.
- Geography and textiles after-school enrichment clubs have helped to increase the profile of both subjects in the Academy.
- Increased publicity of geography at the Academy around the community through the coverage of the fashion show on the Academy website www.belvedereacademy.net.
- Coverage of the fashion show on the Staffordshire Learning Network.

Future developments

Rather than repeat the project too frequently and risk losing impact on the students, the department will, in the future, run the fair trade fashion show once every three years. This way it will run once while each student is in key stage 3. The department also intends to involve key stage 4 students in the choreography for the event, which could lead to a cross-curricular link with GCSE PE. At key stage 5, the involvement of A-level media studies for filming the event and A-level business studies for promotion, ticket sales and organizing local business links, would all be a further potential outcome for the project.

What made the project innovative and creative?

- A real-life and tangible dimension
- The use of external speakers to bring the project to life
- Student autonomy and responsibility to organize a 'live' event
- Cross-curricular and extra-curricular themes and links

In the words of Gavin Sterry, subject leader for geography: 'Bringing in outside speakers and physical products that could be handled and passed around the classroom is not something that we often do – mainly due to time constraints and a very full curriculum. However, this innovative approach was hugely helpful for students in really grasping the issues. In addition, by demonstrating how effective this approach has been, other subject areas have been prompted into bringing in external speakers and even to developing video conferencing'.

Further information

Innovative Geography Teaching Grants www.rgs.org
School website www.belvedereacademy.net

Collaborative, whole-school enrichment

★ *Cardinal Newman Catholic School, Hove, Sussex*

Cardinal Newman Catholic School is a large co-educational 11–18 comprehensive school in Hove, Sussex. The school became a Humanities Specialist College in 2005, received an 'outstanding' Ofsted report in November 2007, and was designated a Training and Development Agency for Schools Training School in September 2009.

The geography department has a reputation of excellence and strives to be 'the best' – contributing to the high-quality learning and teaching within the humanities specialism. At all levels, examination pass rates in geography are above the school and national averages.

The department's vision for geography

The department's vision is to ensure that the geography curriculum is lively, fun, relevant, engaging, stimulating and challenging, and to make sure students are rewarded with high quality attainment relative to their ability.

To make this vision a reality, the department takes a collaborative teamwork approach, engaging all staff and ensuring that their professional development is ongoing.

Within and beyond the school, the department is considered to be:

- Successful and high achieving
- Professional and business-like
- Innovative and risk-taking
- Well managed with strong and visionary leadership
- Award winning (see box).

Awards and other 'marks' of achievement

- GA Secondary Geography Quality Mark 'Centre of Excellence'.
- The department has led on the school's attainment of the International School Award (2008), Eco-Schools Green Flag Award (2008) and Fair Trade Status (2008).
- Sustainable and Healthy Schools, awarded 2008.
- Ordnance Survey Geography Teacher of the Year 2009.
- The Specialist Schools and Academies Trust Cultural Diversity Quality Standard Application 2009–2010 – pending.
- Affiliated to the Prince's Teaching Institute – Geography. The subject leader is the national co-stream coordinator.
- The department leads the local Brighton and Hove Geography Curriculum Network which is supported both by the local authority and the RGS-IBG.
- The department, through the 'Who do we think we are?' project has just secured a business partnership with Dr Nick Barratt and has developed links with the University of Sussex department of geography.
- There are two Chartered Geographers in the department – Maria Larkin (lead teacher for geography) and Graham Goldup (subject leader).

In the words of Graham Goldrup: 'Applying for awards has involved the compilation of portfolios, sometimes with the cooperation and collaboration of other departments across the school, and their submission to the relevant organisations. In some cases funding has been supported from the humanities specialism. There has been assessment and visits from key stakeholders and ongoing updates of progress and renewal. In some cases there have been award ceremonies. There has been a huge investment of time from staff – especially the subject Leader – but this has brought about its own rewards, recognition, funding and further success for the geography department, so the initial investment has been worth it'.

Example: GA SGQM 'Centre of Excellence' award

The school won the Geographical Association's (GA) key stage 3 Secondary Geography Quality Mark (SGQM) 'Centre of Excellence' Award in September 2008.

The quality mark is a framework developed by the GA to enable subject leaders to raise the standards of geography in schools, supporting the teaching of high-quality geography and promoting departmental leadership and management. The framework, based on the whole-school self-evaluation form (SEF), encourages creative and critical thinking and the development of a dynamic and relevant key stage 3 curriculum. The quality mark acts as a 'lever of change' for the development of geography, because it engages all staff in the department in a process of reflection about how well the department is achieving its aims and where its future priorities lie. The whole team takes part in an ongoing process of curriculum review, identifying priorities for departmental CPD and sharing good practice.

The SGQM is awarded at two levels – The Quality Award and a higher 'Centre of Excellence Award'. The Centre of Excellence Award, as received by Cardinal Newman, recognizes the department's contribution to promoting high-quality geography beyond the school and in the local or regional education community.

Example of innovative practice – The geography department leads the way!

Who Do We Think We Are (WDWTWA)? Enrichment Day Programme, 25–26 June 2009

Key stage 3: year 7 and 8 enrichment programme

Curriculum themes: geography, history, citizenship and PSHE

The purpose of the enrichment days were to enhance and raise the profile of the community cohesion aspect of the school, with a view to the school also applying for the Specialist Schools and Academies Trust Cultural Diversity Standard in 2010. The WDWTWA project was an ideal opportunity to get students and teachers to work in a cross-curricular way to think about themselves, their identity and belonging and their place in their communities.

The days were led by the geography department (following attendance at both the British Council and Royal Geographical Society CPD events), but involved the whole school and around 700 pupils.

Based on choice, pupils took part in a series of workshops, relating to the four WDWTWA themes: school and community, faith and belonging, history and settlement and Britishness. Under these four themes, there was a range of activities included, as detailed in Figure 4.3.

School and community A learning trail and guided history of Cardinal Newman School BandBazi Circus – Exploring image and identity through ground skills Producing 'Who Am I? heraldic shields & T-shirt transfers	**Faith and Belonging** 'Five a Day' dance workshop provided by the Springs Dance Company Visits to the Jewish synagogue, the Buddhist Centre, the Brighton Mosque and the Coptic Christian Church to understand similarities and differences between faiths. A visit to the Wintershall Estate, near Guildford to participate in the 'Life of Christ' drama production.
History and Settlement A 'dramatic' tour of the historic Lanes in Brighton with Rob Marks (Actor) Senegalese Drumming Workshop to explore the music and culture of Dakar, Senegal where the school has a Connecting Classrooms link. A day trip to the Natural History Museum to explore the evolution of man and the diversity of species.	**Britishness** Designing and making a Britishness box in art that reflects the students' identity An image and identity workshop based on Britishness provided by Brighton Museum Are we British or European? provided by the modern foreign languages department – A workshop looking at etymology

Figure 4.3 Lesson themes

Prior to the enrichment days, pupils prepared a personal heritage and learning journal, which involved researching the origins of their names (forename and surname), their family roots and their changing community. Students were able to look at the streets that they live on and see how these had changed over time. All students learned about the history of the school and its own heritage journey from a French boarding convent to the comprehensive school that it is today.

In further preparation, pupils also attended lead-in assemblies and, after the workshops, attended a special liturgy based around belonging and caring, community and the prayers of John Henry Newman. At the liturgy, pupils also performed, read and played music to display the skills and outcomes of the workshops; each student contributed something.

Graham Goldup commented: 'This was the best enrichment day programme that we have organized for the year 7 and 8 students with a common theme. All departments and students engaged fully with the concept of WDWTWA, which is central to the values and mission of our work as a Catholic school. The activities were engaging and exciting, very much based around experiential learning and "hands-on experiences". The days have been highly valued and commented upon by the students and there is much visual and display work that has been derived from the two days'.

The importance of Continuing Professional Development

The department considers Continuing Professional Development (CPD) to be of the utmost importance in striving for continual improvement, excellence and innovation, and prides itself on participating in and delivering high-quality national and local CPD. The department participates in CPD offered by the RGS-IBG, the GA, The Prince's Teaching Institute, awarding bodies and other providers.

- All staff are encouraged and supported to participate in CPD. This is linked to their key needs, roles and responsibilities within the department, the departmental priorities and their own performance management targets.
- Recent CPD has, related to delivering the curriculum, new GCSE and A/AS-level specifications, fieldwork in geography, virtual learning environments, outstanding geography learning and teaching, Geographical Information Systems, Google Earth and other relevant

topics. Members of the department have also attended sustainable schools and development education training, and have delivered CPD to wider audiences.

- The department has regular active department meetings that focus on current themes for discussion – for example, underachievement, personal learning and thinking skills, controlled assessment.
- The department also regularly (half-termly) provides CPD opportunities for other geography teachers through the Brighton and Hove Chartered Geography Curriculum Network Meetings.
- The department is also involved, via the subject leader, in geographical events such as the Prince's Teaching Institute School's Programme, and Graham Goldup is a co-stream developer for the Prince's Teaching Institute Summer School at Homerton College Cambridge.
- There are strong links between the geography department at Cardinal Newman and other secondary and primary departments. Graham Goldup and Maria Larkin have run a number of very successful geography conferences for Brighton and Hove.
- Members of the geography department also collaborate on the online Nings and forums (e.g. Staffordshire Learning Network).

Continual improvement

Despite their overwhelming successes, the department continues to strive forward and improve further. Current departmental challenges include:

- Raising the attainment of boys particularly at Levels 6 and 7 in year 9, ongoing monitoring, targeting, whole department INSET and tracking of performance. The department has worked with Alan Kinder, chair of education committee, Geographical Association through QCDA to pilot APP, and student work at Levels 7 and 8 has been showcased on the exemplification of standards website.
- Developing and delivering the schemes of work and the controlled assessment in year 10 with a view to completing year 10 unit exams in summer 2010. This has been developed with CPD, sensible planning and confident application.
- Ensuring that year 13 A-level students are able to attain A grades in summer 2010. There has been a focus on 'stretch and challenge' and developing independent learning.

Lessons for others on innovation and creativity

Cardinal Newman presents an example of creativity and innovation across the board. The department attributes its successes to the following factors:

- Taking a lead and looking for new initiatives and fresh approaches to ensure that geography is always relevant and meaningful.
- Collaborating with other geographers to seek fresh ideas, new approaches and best practice.
- Planning ahead and reviewing departmental position and priorities (GA SGQM helped with this).
- Taking up the opportunities and realizing that anything is possible.
- Staff taking risks and being prepared to trial new styles of learning.

Other schools can learn from their success by:

- Reviewing their own department's progress and development plan and having a long-term vision and goal.
- Pacing yourself and realizing that anything is possible.
- Distributing responsibility and tasks around teaching staff, linked into their performance management.

Further information
School website: www.cncs.co.uk
GA SQM Awards: www.geography.org.uk/11–19/secondaryqualitymark
Who Do We Think We Are?: www.wdwtwa.org.uk

A whole-school approach to sustainability

★ *Currie Community High School, Edinburgh, Scotland*

Currie Community High School provides secondary education for approximately 900 pupils. It has a broad community education programme for adults and children, being used extensively outside of school hours. In addition, the school has a long-standing commitment to environmental education and now to sustainable development education (SDE). To date, their achievements in this area have been marked by a number of prestigious awards (see Figure 4.4).

Sustainability at Currie High is clearly integrated into the very fabric of the school. Here, sustainability enjoys real commitment-from senior management: the head teacher, a deputy head teacher and the business manager are all fully involved in driving the agenda forward, and the school also employs an environmental projects coordinator. This top-down commitment is coupled with a heavy emphasis on student voice – on pupil engagement, involvement and ownership of the sustainability of the school. A number of pupil groups have been established, supported by teaching and support staff, to look at areas such as energy consumption and generation, school grounds and biodiversity, and waste reduction.

It is this two-tiered approach that ensures sustainability is embedded into the curriculum and ethos of the school, as well as encouraging 'buy-in' from pupils.

Examples of sustainable achievements

Energy education programme The school has a clearly defined and structured energy education programme that permeates all aspects of the curriculum. For example, in science, pupils investigate the pros and cons of different energy sources in the generation of electricity.

S1 SDE course (equivalent to year 7) In 2003, Currie High School, in partnership with the Worldwide Fund for nature, developed an SDE course called 'Tracks through Time' for all S1 pupils. Pupils learn about major sustainability issues today, look back at the way people lived 50 years ago and then imagine life 50 years into the future, in order to consider what changes need to be made to make the future more sustainable. The course provides a basic understanding of the concept of sustainability for all pupils and is built on in subsequent years. The course is discrete and studied for one hour per week over 18 weeks.

Eco-Schools programme It is very important to both teach about sustainability issues and provide opportunities for pupils to take action to reduce the environmental impact of the school. This has been implemented at Currie High through the framework of the Eco-Schools programme. Through this, pupils undertake an environmental review, identify and discuss points for action and, together with staff, an action plan is formulated. Pupils are involved in its implementation, monitoring and evaluation, and communication with the rest of the school. The school was awarded its third Eco-Schools Green Flag in 2009.

Tracking and monitoring energy consumption A pupil-led energy group monitors energy consumption using electricity monitoring meters, and by accessing available figures for gas and electricity consumption. Currently, an electronic information system is being installed which will record both energy consumption and generation as well as weather parameters. This will enable better access to data for pupil energy monitoring and curricular use in physics, geography, maths and IT. This will soon be available on the internet for others to use.

Sustainable technologies The school has adopted a range of sustainable technologies, including a wind turbine, solar thermal panels, high-efficiency lighting, and insulation to combat heat loss. The combination of behavioural changes and installation of new technologies has led to an overall saving for the school of around £12,500 per year and 70 tonnes of carbon dioxide.

Global school partnership In 2004, Currie High formed a partnership with Chogoria Girls' High School in Kenya, and staff and pupils from both schools have undertaken reciprocal visits. The personal contact, exchange of information and work on shared curricular projects has brought to life issues relating to the developing world and gives a real and personal focus to pupils' work. Projects include:

- Pupils from several year groups researching renewable energy technologies suitable for Scotland or Kenya and exchanging this information.
- Pupils compiling a booklet about their own school and exchanging these.
- Designing a mask or jewellery based on a theme of African life and culture using visual stimuli from Chogoria.
- Undertaking conservation work in a local woodland in Currie and in the forest by Chogoria and comparing the aims and methods used.

This work has been supported by the Department for International Development's Global Schools Partnership Curriculum Grant.

School grounds and biodiversity The school grounds have been developed for both teaching and amenity use. In the 'outdoor classroom', pupils are taught about food webs, human dependence on the environment to sustain life, some plant classification, the basics of plant evolution and methods of pollination, for example.

For over 20 years, pupils and staff have also been responsible for the rescue and conservation of 'Roley's Wood', a strip of ancient woodland adjacent to the school. Trees have been planted all around the school campus to create a wildlife corridor linking Roley's Wood with other small areas of woodland in Currie. For more information and some resources and activities, go to www.currieecology.org.uk.

Waste minimization The '3 Rs' (reduce, reuse and recycle) are very important at Currie High, and the school works to minimize waste. It does this in a number of ways, for example:

- **Paper recycling** – a rota of S1 and S2 pupils collect and weigh paper from around the school, during registration on Wednesdays. Last year alone, 3,275kg of paper were sent for recycling.
- **Reusing waste in art** – several projects within the art curriculum are undertaken using 'waste' materials. In 2009–10, pupils designed and made various clothes re-using materials and incorporating 'waste' items. Subsequently, a fashion show was held where pupils successfully modelled their creations.

The energy group in action

The group includes pupil representatives from S2 (year 8), S3 (year 9) and S6 (year 12). Several members of the group are from the advanced higher physics class and some from the eco-committee.

In October 2008, the energy group conducted a survey of classrooms, during lunchtimes and after school, in order to record if lights had been switched off in unoccupied rooms. Pupils found that lights were left on in 25 per cent of unoccupied rooms. The results were fed back to staff, and the survey was repeated in January 2009, when it was found that the figure had been reduced to 20 per cent. This 5 per cent reduction translates to a saving of £530 for the academic year. The survey is repeated periodically to remind staff to switch off lights in order to reduce energy use.

In addition, the group researched tips on energy saving relevant to young people. These tips were read from the daily bulletin to all pupils in the school for one week in November 2008, and were also displayed on the Eco-Schools notice board. Following this, tutor groups were asked to discuss the need to save energy, and pupils and staff were asked to make a pledge to save energy in their own lifestyles. Pledges were recorded and re-visited one month later, and respondents were asked to record whether it was easy or difficult. Most people reported that it was easy to make the savings they had pledged, and many said that it was just a question of forming the habit.

What next?

Considerable progress has been made to raise awareness and make the school more sustainable, but it is recognized there is much still to be done. The school is currently working to improve cross-curricular links in several topics, and plans for the coming year include:

- A video diary celebrating the biodiversity of the school grounds for the International Year of Biodiversity.
- A new inter-disciplinary project between biology and geography on climate change, involving work with Chogoria High School.
- The creation of a school fruit orchard.

Award	**Date**
Eco-School's – Green Flag Award	2004, 2007, 2009
Standard Life achievement Award	Highly commended for their submission on 'Powering and Empowering for a Sustainable Future' 2009
Royal Zoological Society Environmental Award	2007 joint winners 'Hands across Continents'
The Ashden Award for sustainable energy	2009 joint winners

Figure 4.4 Awards received by Currie High School

Lessons for other schools on sustainability

Currie High School's work on sustainability is clearly innovative and ground-breaking in a range of areas. Their success, however, can be emulated by others. The school attributes its success largely to the following:

- Commitment and involvement of the senior management team.
- Dedication and commitment from a range of other staff (including non-teaching staff).
- Embedding of sustainability across most areas of the curriculum.
- Provision of opportunities for pupils to have a 'voice' and take practical action.
- Use of real-life case studies, via links and partnerships with schools abroad.
- Use of real data in order to built upon and enrich curriculum topics.

Further information

There are a number of awards, quality marks, schemes, grants and funding streams available to schools who want to become more sustainable. For more information, see the websites in Figure 4.5.

Organisation	URL
Ashden School Award	www.ashdenawards.org
EcoSchools	www.eco-schools.org.uk
Carbon Trust	www.carbontrust.co.uk
NEF (National Energy Foundation)	www.nef.org.uk
Envirowise	www.envirowise.gov.uk
Energy Saving Trust	www.energysavingtrust.org.uk
Friends of the Earth	www.foe.co.uk
BRE	www.bre.co.uk
British Council for School Environments	www.bcse.uk.net

Figure 4.5 Website addresses

For more detailed information about Currie Community High School and their work on sustainability, visit their website at www.curriechs.co.uk.

Creativity in the classroom – 'School of the air'

★ *Stopsley High School, Luton*

Stopsley High School is an 11–16 mixed comprehensive Specialist Sports School in Luton, Bedfordshire, with approximately 900 learners on its roll. The school has many successes to be proud of – the most recent Ofsted report (2007) was good with outstanding features, and the head teacher's vision is to establish the school as a centre of excellence, working closely and creatively with their partners and community.

The geography department is equally successful – marked by the award of the Geographical Association's Centre of Excellence and the Quality Mark for Secondary Geography (SGQM) in September 2008. See page 127 for further details on the award. The team is made up of five staff, and among them there are many talents. The head of the department, Louise Ellis, is Regional Subject Adviser, Chartered Geographer, Teacher Consultant for the GA and author of a *GA KS3 Toolkit – A Thorny Issue*.

The department's vision for geography

Geography is 'living'. We are a part of 'geography'. Hence, we start in the classroom situation with the known and move towards the unknown. We endeavour to develop an awareness of and an interest in people, place and the environment from the personal to the global. While undertaking this we aim to establish an innovative, creative and enjoyable approach to our work.

The department has adopted a whole raft of creative teaching and learning methods to enthuse and engage its pupils and to stimulate their interest in geography. Figure 4.6 shows some of the assessment methods used across key stages and a range of topics.

Examples of assessment methods	
Advertisement	Ministerial Directive
Argument	Newspaper report
Card sort	Phone call
Charades	Poem/Rap
Chart/table/graph	Postcard
Charter	Poster
Coded message	Recipe
Conversation	Shadow play
Design a game	Shopping list
Experiment	Story
Fact File	System diagram
Five Day Diary	Venn diagram
Letter to the Editor	

Figure 4.6 Assessment methods

Example of innovative and creative practice

Project title: School of the air (Alice Springs) – A Geographical Enquiry
Key stage 3/year 7
Unit of study: Place, space, scale

The school of the air module was used by the school as part of the GA Making Geography Happen project.

This project fits into a wider scheme of work for year 7:

- Personal geography unit – I am, yet who am I? (place, space, scale)
- School of the air (place, space, scale)
- Toy story (environmental interaction, interdependence)
- Dr who (physical and human processes)
- Geography in the news.

Geographical enquiry: school of the air

How long does it take you to get to school each morning?
Imagine having a 10-hour drive to school. How would you, your family and the local community cope with this situation?

Motivating and enthusing learners

The initial enquiry question formed the motivational 'hook' and awoke the pupils' enthusiasm. Their attention was focused through the design of a range of activities that challenged learners in a fun and creative way, for example, 'think of the link' activity, jigsaw task, the opportunity of model making, and the creative use of music and film.

Assessment choices

1. A TV documentary on the school of the air is to be produced for the BBC. As a researcher for the BBC you have flown out to Alice Springs to interview staff and children. Produce a transcript of an interview with one teacher and one pupil.
2. You attend the school of the air. Your new home tutor from England arrives in six weeks. Write a letter to your tutor to tell her/him about your home and school life.
3. Produce a leaflet for the many tourists who visit the school of the air information centre. The leaflet will give a wide range of information – What? Where? Why? When? How?
4. Model making: you could make someone like me and just cover me with information about the school of the air. What? Where? Why? When? How?

Pupil assessment strategy

An assessment strategy has been adopted across the key stage, for all assignments. Pupils follow this strategy consistently and are involved at all stages in assessing their own learning and performance (Figure 4.7).

Pupil progression

Pupils were provided with a range of interesting methods to reflect together on what they learned. This was done through 'Reflection Logs' and 'Reflection Blobs'.

Example, Reflection log

- What have you learned today?
- How have you learned?
- What went well? Why?
- What did not go well? Why?
- What did you enjoy? Why?
- What did you not enjoy? Why?
- If you did this again, what would you do differently?

Stage	Task
Stage 1	Portfolio – folder provided for each learner to retain their assessments and record cards for key stage 3
Stage 2	Planning sheet – completed by each learner when embarking on an assignment, providing opportunities for peer and self-assessment
Stage 3	Pupil comment bank – comment bank for the teacher to aid the marking of assignments. These include both positive comments and 'mission statements' to support target setting
Stage 4	Record card – bi-polar style record card of National Curriculum levels awarded for assignments
Stage 5	Pupil assessment – pupil assignments
Stage 6	Reflection log – debriefs undertaken at the end of each module

Figure 4.7 Assessment strategy

Teacher reflection

The teacher's reflection on the assignments was that it clearly showed evidence of:

- Creative, critical independent learning.
- Development of geographical knowledge, understanding and skills.
- A grasp of the 5 Ws and the use of the personalized structure for assignments: issue, location, scale, events.
- The opportunity to develop skills: for example, the ability to make informed decisions using geographical evidence.
- An understanding of 'similarities and differences' between 'our place' and one other in a different location.
- The application and understanding of concepts such as place, space and scale.
- Children having fun and enjoying the learning process in geography.

Lessons for others on innovation and creativity

The department's approach to learning is clearly innovative and vibrant, and they attribute much of their success to the creative vision of staff within the department. Head of department Louise Ellis gives her advice to others – be open minded, creative and daring! She says: 'You have to be creative yourself, I think. I firmly believe that all geographers are capable of this but it takes time to develop this approach, not only in creating resources, but also in delivery style. You have to be motivated, you need IT skills such as using PowerPoint and you need to be prepared to give things time. Creative activities take a long time to prepare, but they can cover several weeks work and you then have them as a permanent resource. You have to dare to move away from the tradition of text books. Be open-minded. Be prepared to take risks. Just have a go!'

Further information

Visit the Stopsley High School's website http://uca.digitalbrain.com/e2bn/leas/u99/schools/uca/frontpage/home/

Louise Ellis, Head of Department at Stopsley High School is author of: Key stage 3 Geography Teachers' Toolkit: *A Thorny Issue, Should I Buy a Valentine's Rose?* (Sheffield: Geographical Association, 2009).

Task 4.1: Learning from the case studies

Once you have read through the case studies, reflect on them by answering the following questions:

- What common principles have teachers in the case studies used to create outstanding learning opportunities?
- What things do they have in common with your own teaching?
- What stands out as *different* from what you currently do in your classroom?
- Identify what seems to stand out as the most important principle in the case studies that you do not currently address. Consider how you might build this in to your teaching in the next half-term. Who will need to help you as you do this, and what will their role be?
- At the end of the next half-term, review your work again. How well did things go? What were the barriers to implementing your actions, and what work remains to be done?

5 Taking things further

Overview

This chapter explains where geography teachers can go for further support and guidance on a wealth of issues relating to their role. It includes details of recommended resources for geography teaching: books, magazines, the web, hands-on resources and ICT tools, each annotated to show strengths. There are also details of professional associations and societies to join and where else to go for help to create a network of support from the local to the national, including funding ideas.

Books

Every geography department should have a comprehensive CPD library of books to inspire, enthuse and motivate teachers. The following annotated selection of books represents, in the author's opinion, some of the essential titles for inclusion in your CPD library.

Bailey, P. and Fox, P. (1997), *The Geography Teachers' Handbook*. Sheffield: Geographical Association.

- A compendium of invaluable information for teachers of geography from the trusted stable of the Geographical Association.

Best, B. J. (2003), *The Accelerated Learning Pocketbook*. Alresford: Teachers' Pocketbooks.

- Explains in easily digestible chunks the principles of accelerated learning and is full of practical lesson advice.

Best, B., and Thomas, W. (2007), *The Creative Teaching & Learning Toolkit*. London: Continuum International Publishing.

- Explains the principles of creative teaching and learning, with lots of examples of lesson activities.

—(2008), *The Creative Teaching & Learning Resource Book*. London: Continuum International Publishing.

- Over 100 practical lesson activities that promote creative teaching and learning.

Black, P., Harrison, C., Lee, C., Marshall, B. & William, D. (2003), *Assessment for Learning: Putting It into Practice*. Maidenhead: Open University Press.

- The best text on assessment for learning.

Leat, D., and Chandler, S. (1998), *Thinking Through Geography*. Cambridge: Chris Kington Publishing.

Nichols, A., Kinninment, D., and Leat, D. (2000), *More Thinking through Geography*. Cambridge: Chris Kington Publishing.

- These two invaluable volumes are full of thought-provoking lesson activities that promote students' thinking.

Marshall, L., and Rowland, F. (1993), *A Guide to Learning Independently*. Maidenhead: Open University Press.

- Contains detailed advice on independent learning.

Powell, A. (1997), *Handbook of Post-16 Geography*. Sheffield: Geographical Association.

- Specific advice on teaching post-16 students in geography.

Wallace, B., Maker, J., and Cave, D. (2005), *Thinking Skills and Problem-solving – an Inclusive Approach: A Practical Guide for Teachers in Primary Schools.* Oxford: NACE/David Fulton Publishers.

- An excellent introduction to the fascinating world of TASC, which stands for Thinking Actively in a Social Context. It is a method of working that is especially appropriate to geography students. Although this book is written for primary school teachers, it has much relevance for key stage 3 and 4 teaching.

Wood, P., Hymer, B., and Michel, D. (2007), *Dilemma-based Learning in the Humanities: Integrating Social, Emotional and Thinking Skills.* Cambridge: Chris Kington Publishing.

- A very useful book that contains many worked examples and makes extensive links to thinking skills, philosophy for children and other aspects of learning.

Wragg, E., and Brown, G. (2001), *Questioning in the Secondary School.* Oxford: Routledge Falmer.

- An excellent text on questioning strategies.

Magazines

BBC Focus magazine – published monthly
BBC Wildlife Magazine – published monthly
Geographical Magazine – published monthly
National Geographic – published monthly
Teaching Geography – published quarterly

Websites

There is a wealth of superb internet sites for the study of geography: so many, in fact, that you could devote a whole book to the subject. The following annotated selection represents some of the top internet sites for geography-related learning.

★ *BBC geography: secondary*

www.bbc.co.uk/schools/websites/11_16/site/geography.shtml

This site brings with it the trusted brand of the BBC, and the site is a good place to go to find lesson ideas. There is also a very useful 'Bitesize' revision section for students.

★ *Carbon detectives' kit*

www.carbondetectiveseurope.org

This site contains an online carbon footprint detector designed to help students understand key issues relating to climate change. Students can also learn what their school can do to improve its sustainability credentials.

★ *CIA world factbook*

www.cia.gov/library/publications/the-world-factbook/index.html

The Central Intelligence Agency's World Factbook provides information on the history, people, government, economy, geography, communications, transportation, military, and transnational issues for 266 world entities. Constantly updated, the site is a mine of useful information for use in geography lessons and in student research projects.

★ *Climate for classrooms*

http://climate4classrooms.org/en

Provides high-quality free teaching resources on climate change for students age 11 and up. The site includes interactive data sets showing the latest global and national climate predictions; climate science brought to life by the experts; and case studies investigating global, national, and local impacts and solutions. There is also guidance for teachers on how to use all these resources.

★ *Cloud appreciation society*

www.cloudappreciationsociety.org

A wonderful idiosyncratic site full of superb photos of clouds and atmospheric phenomena and a site to go for inspiration when planning weather and climate work. The site contains many fantastic images that can be used to attract students' attention at the start of lessons.

★ *Digital geography*

www.digitalgeography.co.uk

A site maintained by advanced skills teacher Noel Jenkins which focuses on using new technologies as part of the geography curriculum. Information is clearly organized, and the content includes an interesting range of pod movies.

★ *Geograph*

www.geograph.org.uk

This ambitious project has its aim to collect representative photos of every 1km grid square in Britain and Ireland. A visit to any area produces a photo mosaic which gives a real sense of place. Ideal for starter activities and for students to gain a visual representation of the places they are studying.

★ *Geographical association*

www.geography.org.uk

The GA's website is a great place to go to gain practical support for organizing your geography curriculum and for lesson activities. You'll need to be a member of the GA to access some parts of the site. An excellent feature of the site is the inclusion of resources and lesson ideas linked to current affairs. There is also information on grants for geography teachers plus term quizzes for students. See also the Planet Sport website below.

★ *Geography all the way*

www.geographyalltheway.com

This is Richard Allaway's critically acclaimed site, with a wealth of superb learning resources. The site uses ingenious talking heads to guide users through a series of mini enquiries. Another innovative feature of the site is a weekly 'where in the world' quiz which features a photograph which visitors need to work out where in the world it was taken.

★ *Geography at the movies*

www.gatm.org.uk

This site contains free video resources for geography teachers. It is a place to go to access and share videos which can used to enliven geography lessons. The videos are arranged into categories.

★ *Geography dictionary and glossary*

www.tuition.com.hk/geography

This is perhaps the internet's most comprehensive dictionary and glossary for students, with over 1,400 terms defined, all cross referenced. An ideal place for students to go to gain concise definitions of all the terms they are likely to come across and ideal for building up their own personal dictionary (see page 102).

★ *Geography in the news*

www.geographyinthenews.rgs.org

This subscription-only site, hosted by the Royal Geographical Society, provides some wonderful resources linked to everyday events around the world. Using the site will help you to bring geography alive for your students.

★ *Geography on the internet*

www.geography.learnontheinternet.co.uk

A very useful and long-established site for geography teachers and students. There are lots of online activities, separate parts of the site aimed at key stage 3 and GCSE students, some excellent videos and host of other useful content. The online A–Z of geography-related websites is definitely an area to bookmark for your Virtual Learning Environment (VLE).

★ *Geography pages*

www.geographypages.co.uk

One of the best geography portal sites on the web, with links to hundreds of sites that will enrich the teaching of the subject. A 'must-add' addition to your geography VLE.

★ *The geography site*

www.geography-site.co.uk

Contains hundreds of resources to aid the teaching of the subject, plus an excellent image gallery of almost 1,000 images to use in lessons, homework and wall displays.

★ *Geography teaching today*

www.geographyteachingtoday.org.uk

This is the website of the Geography Action Plan, which is seeking to raise the profile of geography teaching in primary and secondary schools. There are some excellent lesson ideas on the site, together with the news of training events that are free for geography teachers. You can also use the site to find out about Geography Ambassadors who will come into your school to be a champion for the subject.

★ *Geointeractive*

www.geointeractive.co.uk

Contains over 1,000 free resources donated by teachers from across the United Kingdom, plus a wide range of links and other useful information. An excellent collection of resources to use in your lessons, with many starting points for exciting learning journeys.

★ *Georesources*

www.georesources.co.uk

An award-winning portal site with hundreds of lessons ideas and links to the world of geography. An interesting feature of the site is the inclusion of four virtual fieldwork units.

★ *Geotube*

www.geotubevideos.co.uk

A wonderful collection of over 1,000 videos for geography teachers to use. The videos are arranged in five channels: environmental, physical, social, economic and other. You can get seven days of access free; after this time, you need to donate £10 to charity to continue to gain access to the videos.

★ *Global gateway*

www.globalgateway.org

This is the site to visit if you want to form a link with a school in another country in order to carry out collaborative work. This site also contains comprehensive support material to help you get the best from your international links.

★ *Global eye*

www.globaleye.org.uk

Winner of a Geographical Association Gold Award, the Global Eye website is based on the magazine of the same name and focuses on international development and environmental issues. The site includes teachers' resources and indices for countries and themes. This site is a wonderful source of articles which can be used with students.

★ *Google earth*

http://earth.google.com

Arguably the best mapping website, Google earth offers a wealth of opportunities to use digital mapping and aerial photography in the classroom.

★ *Juicy geography*

www.juicygeography.co.uk

A wonderful collection of ideas, lessons and resources for geography teachers and assembled by advanced skills teacher Noel Jenkins. Noel has put together a very stimulating site which is certainly one to bookmark for frequent visits.

★ *Key stage 3 schemes of work*

www.standards.dfes.gov.uk/schemes2/secondary_geography/?view=get

Part of the standards site, this very useful resource gives schemes of work for each of the 24 units of the key stage 3 syllabus, with specific learning objectives and lesson ideas. The site also shows you how you can make links to other subject areas in an especially detailed part of the site, as well as containing advice on sequencing the units.

★ *London grid for learning*

http://cms.lgfl.net/web/lgfl/geography

This site contains some very useful resources to aid geographical learning, including some detailed project-based materials. A recent addition to the site is an extensive set of resources on managing nuclear waste, which culminates in a decision-making exercise.

★ *The Met Office*

www.metoffice.gov.uk

Far more than just a place to go to find out about tomorrow's weather, the Met Office website is a mine of useful information and background resources that can be used to enrich the teaching of weather and climate. Of topical interest are special features about the weather forecast for major sporting and other events. The satellite images on the site are especially useful.

★ *National association for environmental education*

www.naee.org.uk

A charity dedicated to promoting the cause of environmental education. Their website contains a selection of articles from their journal *Environmental Education* as well as a very useful selection of links to other environmental websites. You can become a member of the association, which then entitles you to free copies of the journal and the opportunity to attend conferences and meetings.

★ *National Geographic*

http://ngm.nationalgeographic.com

National Geographic's award-winning website, with a wealth of articles and learning resources for teachers and students. One of the major strengths of the site is the superb collection of high-quality photos which can be used in presentations to students or by the students themselves in their work.

★ *National Geographic map machine*

http://maps.nationalgeographic.com/maps

This is probably the best world mapping site on the web, with the facility to select any country in the world and display a map with the national flag and other factual information such as population, capital, main religions, languages, literacy rate and life expectancy. There is also information on the country's history and economy. More recently, a new feature has been introduced, called 'View From Above', which shows maps of countries based on satellite photographs.

★ *National Hurricane center*

www.nhc.noaa.gov

The home of the US National Hurricane Center, this site is a superb place to find out about the latest tropical storms and hurricanes. There is also extensive information about preparing for hurricanes, as well as historical information on past hurricanes and their paths.

★ *Ordnance survey mapping*

www.ordnancesurvey.co.uk/oswebsite/opendata

The ordnance survey open data mapping site provides some of the most detailed and accurate mapping available for the United Kingdom. You can zoom in to any location in the country or search using place name, postcode or grid reference. Great for developing your students' mapwork skills.

★ *Ordnance survey mapzone*

http://mapzone.ordnancesurvey.co.uk/mapzone/index.html

This is a fun site for students to learn about mapping. There is a range of challenges and games offered, including a very useful GIS simulator programme which introduces the benefits of GIS through a real-life decision-making exercise. This is a site which is sure to entertain and educate your students.

★ *Planet Sport*

www.geography.org.uk/projects/planetsport

A website which contains resources linking geographical themes – such as regeneration, economic development and tourism – with global sporting events. This is an ideal site to visit to acquire resources which help to engage students who may not traditionally be interested in geography.

★ *Royal Geographical Society*

www.rgs.org

The website of the United Kingdom's learned society for geographers, packed with useful information and links of use to geography teachers. Of special interest is the grants section of the website which outlines some of the funding opportunities aimed at geography teachers. See also Geography in the news above.

★ *Staffordshire Learning Network*

www.sln.org.uk/geography

Widely regarded as the best local-authority maintained geography site, the Staffordshire Learning Network offers a host of excellent resources to spice up your geography lessons. There are also some extremely useful forums where you can discuss anything from Ofsted inspections to job opportunities.

★ *The Tornado Project*

www.tornadoproject.com

A useful site to learn about tornadoes and their effects. This site has lots to interest students, including a stark set of 'tornado stories' which tell of the dramatic impact of tornadoes on people.

★ *Teachers' TV: geography*

www.teachers.tv/subjects/secondary/geography

Containing a databank of videos from the archives of Teachers' TV, this site comes from a trusted name in educational resources. A useful feature of the site is the ability to search by keywords.

★ *US Geological Survey: volcanoes*

http://volcanoes.usgs.gov

Probably the finest volcano site on the web, this resource provides a wealth of information about the world of volcanism. The site contains details of all currently erupting volcanoes, resources for teachers and frequently asked questions about volcanoes. An engaging feature is a series of webcams from active volcano sites around the world. The site represents a rich source of information for both students and staff wanting to know more about volcanoes.

★ *Worldwide earthquake locator*

http://tsunami.geo.ed.ac.uk/local-bin/quakes/mapscript/home.pl

This dynamic site, produced by the University of Edinburgh, aims to provide up-to-date information and detailed dynamic maps of earthquakes across the world within a maximum of 24 hours of their occurrence. You can see earthquake predictions, view an animation of recent quakes and learn about the very latest quakes around the world.

ICT tools

The following selection of ICT tools represents a small sample of the myriad of programmes available that enrich the teaching of geography. The programmes listed represent tried-and-tested tools for geographical learning. Note that there are many free resources online which are perfectly adequate for use with students, and it is not necessary to spend large sums of money in order to equip your department with expensive branded products.

- Students should have access to a content generator programme that enables them to create content and place it on the school's VLE. There are some excellent free programmes available on the web.
- Students should also have access to a video editing programme to make the most of digital video and images. A programme that includes the ability to generate animations should be used. Again, there are many good free examples available on the web.
- Two of the best GIS programmes are ESRI UK's Digital Worlds package and Aegis 3's Success Guides. Both have the potential to open up the huge possibilities of GIS programmes to your students.
- The company Birchfield (www.birchfield.co.uk) produces some excellent classroom resources for geography in the form of curriculum content, activities and games. These range from resources on fragile environments to weather and climate. There is a very useful programme which includes nine geographical games for whiteboards, which is ideal for starters and plenaries.

- The company Boardworks (www.boardworks.co.uk) has worked hard to improve its offerings to geography teachers in recent years. Their toolkit product for fieldwork is particularly recommended.
- Scamp 4 (produced by Pebbleshore Ltd; www.pebbleshore.co.uk) – this CD-ROM is an interactive GIS mapping programme containing census data. It enables much of the 2001 census data to be displayed using a variety of different methods and scales. The CD-ROM is enhanced by the use of OS raster master for selected locations at a scale of 1:250,000 on which census data can be superimposed.
- There are an increasing number of applications (or 'apps') now available for smart phones (often free or very cheap), many of which have the potential to add impact to your lessons. New apps are being launched all the time, so it is well worth keeping track of new releases to see what they could offer for your geography teaching.

Hands-on resources

There are some excellent games and other hands-on resources which can support your work as a geography teacher. Three personal favourites are included below:

- *The Chocolate game* – introducing the idea of fair trade in a fun and engaging way (available online at www.learn.christianaid.org.uk/YouthLeaderResources/choc_trade.aspx).
- *Tools for logovisual thinking* (see page 85) – reusable hands-on equipment to help see what you are thinking, available from www.logovisual.com.
- *Global steps* – an excellent card game which helps you calculate how many earths would be needed if everybody consumed the same resources as you. For more information, see www.bestfootforward.com/globalsteps.

Professional associations and societies

★ *Geographical association*

www.geography.org.uk

The society which supports the work of geography teachers in schools and colleges, publishing several learned journals as well as the invaluable *Teaching Geography* magazine.

★ *Geology society*

www.geolsoc.org

Offers Fellowship opportunities for geography teachers who have a specialist interest in the geological side of the subject. There is also the option to become a Chartered Geologist. A range of publications are produced by the society.

★ *Royal geographical society*

www.rgs.org

Offers Fellowship opportunities and the chance to gain the status of Chartered Geographer. The RGS also publishes a range of printed journals, including the excellent *Geographical Magazine*.

★ *Royal meteorological society*

www.rmets.org

The national society for teachers interested in weather and climate. The website includes an excellent section of educational resources called MetLink, with details of weather; and a curriculum, lesson plans and lots of climate and weather resources. The site also contains annotated links to many other climate and weather websites.

Selected funding sources

The following websites fast-track you to some of the best funding sources for school-based geography teaching and geography enrichment activities. It is also worth investigating some of the excellent subscription-based websites which can provide very detailed information on funding sources from their vast databases. The best three are www.funderfinder.org.uk (offers cut price charges for 24-hour access), www.grantfinder.co.uk and www.grants4schools.info (offers a free trial).

Bear in mind that almost all funders want you to add something new to the curriculum and will not simply fund the purchase of textbooks and other standard classroom equipment. If you are seeking funds for such things, then there are some specific funding sources which can help you generate cash (see 'Funds for income generation' below). You can also raise funds through the staging of fundraising events such as sponsored walks and similar activities.

Before you embark on any attempts to gain funding from the following sources, it is wise to speak first with your school's fund-raising coordinator (or, failing that, business manager/bursar). This person is likely to understand the bidding process and should be able to provide very helpful advice on submitting bids. Some local authorities also employ a fundraising manager who, again, would be an invaluable person to talk to.

Some of the charitable trusts mentioned are best approached in tandem with another department at your school, or through a single whole school application which includes specific benefits for the geography department. These are indicated in the listings.

You can increase the number of grant schemes which your school can apply to by channelling your application through the PTA of schools' friends' groups, if these have charitable status. This is because some funders will only donate to registered charities.

★ *Awards for all*

www.awardsforall.org.uk

Up to £10,000 is available for projects which add something new to the curriculum. The aim of the scheme is to support small, local community-based projects which bring benefits to a wide range of people. When applying for these awards, it is helpful to think in terms of a geography project which can involve other members of the community. Applications can be submitted any time.

- *Example*: a school received a £5,400 grant in order to publish a geography trail leaflet which guided people around the geographical features of the local town. The leaflet was given out to local residents.

★ *British Ecological Society innovation in ecological education grants*

www.britishecologicalsociety.org/grants/education/iee.php

The British Ecological Society is a charity which aims to promote and foster the study of ecology. Its Innovation in Ecological Education Grant scheme is to help teachers to develop creative and innovative approaches in communicating ecology to young people. Funds can also be used to evaluate the teaching of ecology. Projects can be based inside or outside the classroom. As ecology and the study of ecosystems and habitats forms part of the geography syllabus, especially at A level, this is a scheme that can be used to enrich the teaching of the subject. Up to £1,500 is available to successful schools, and there are two deadline for bids: 15 March and 15 September.

- *Example*: a school received an award of £1,500 to investigate how studies into the ecology and conservation of a wild flower meadow can be enhanced by the used of notebook computers. Three notebook computers were purchased and loaded with plant and bird identification software for use in and outside the classroom. Also loaded were web pages on the ecology and conservation of wild flower meadows. The teacher monitored the use of the notebook computers during the unit of study on the wild flower meadow, and students were asked to give feedback on how useful the notebooks had been.

★ *Calouste Gulbenkian Foundation*

www.gulbenkian.org.uk

This is a major grant-making trust which has made awards to schools in the past. Its Innovation Fund is currently the main fund to apply to; this aims to fund genuinely innovative ideas and partnerships across cultural, education and social interests. Priority will be given to projects that best meet the organization's strategic aims, namely cultural understanding, fulfilling potential and environment. Funding is available in the range £10,000 to £25,000. Initial ideas can be submitted at any time; if short listed, further information will be sought. The fact that this find makes large donations means that it would be a good idea to team up with another department to make a joint bid, or even make one bid on behalf of the whole school. You would also be well advised to include some community element in your bid.

- *Example*: a school was given £12,000 to set up a virtual classroom in a youth centre to educate disaffected students.

★ *Comenius awards*

www.britishcouncil.org/comenius-schools.htm

Up to £25,000 is available to support collaborative projects between schools in the United Kingdom and those in other parts of Europe. The funding available is designed to support work on cross-curricular projects and covers study visits, which can include students. This is an ideal funding source which can be applied for in partnership with colleagues in other departments at your school, with the aim of carrying out project work that compliments various departmental syllabuses. Applications can be submitted any time.

- *Example*: a school was given a £15,000 grant to support an environmentally themed exchange visit with a school in Brittany. The students produced a bilingual book on the environment in their home area.

★ *Ernest Cook Trust*

www.ernestcooktrust.org.uk

This trust fund provides grants to schools and other not-for-profit organizations wishing to encourage young people's interest either in the countryside and the environment, the arts, or aiming to raise levels of literacy and numeracy. There are two main schemes: a small ground programme for awards of up to £4,000 (deadlines are bimonthly) and a large programme for awards of over £4,000 (deadlines 31 January and 31 July).

- *Example*: a school received a grant of £2,000 to build a weather station which encouraged the students to work together to gather data and 'own' the equipment.

★ *Esmee Fairbairn Foundation*

www.esmeefairbairn.org.uk

One of the largest grant-giving bodies in the United Kingdom, with over £20 million given to projects annually. The Foundation has awarded several schools grants for projects which have a strong community element. One of the current strands that the charity is keen to support is research into teaching and learning approaches that address current challenges in schools for which large grants of up £250,000 are available (though schools are likely to bid for much less than this!). This is an ideal fund to apply to, in collaboration with another department at your school, or to make one application on behalf of the whole school.

- *Example*: a school was awarded £6,000 to run a fair trade awareness week, which included extensive collaboration with the local branch of Oxfam. Students got involved in a range of hands-on activities while learning about fair trade and its implications for their lives, and members of the local community were invited into school to see the outcomes of the week.

★ *Fawcett fellowships*

www.geog.ucl.ac.uk/admissions-and-teaching/information-for-schools/introduction

These fellowships are designed to enable UK-based teachers in mid career to study at University College London (UCL) for a term. Applicants should develop their own plan of how to spend the time: for example, bringing themselves up to date with aspects of the discipline, exploring new teaching fields, developing new skills, or preparing new teaching materials. Fellows have full access to the library and IT resources at UCL, and to the expertise of its geography staff. They should then return to their permanent jobs – refreshed and ready to stimulate others. The funding is available to fund supply teaching cover for the duration of the fellowship. The fellowships offer a very valuable CPD opportunity for secondary school geography teachers. The deadline for applications is 30 April each year.

★ *First Light*

www.firstlightonline.co.uk

First Light is an organization that funds and inspires the making of short films, reflecting the diversity of young people's lives. This is an organization to apply to if you are interested using film on a geographical theme to inspire your students. There is a wide range of different funding schemes to apply to, with the amount of money available typically being in the low thousands of pounds.

- *Example*: a school received £3,000 for a film that explored local people's attitude to a woodland that was threatened with demolition for a new housing estate.

★ *Foyle Foundation*

www.foylefoundation.org.uk

This is a charitable trust which has had a good record of supporting schools over recent years. Grants are available of between £5,000 and £20,000 for projects that are based on learning, arts or health, with precedence given to projects that make a difference because funding is difficult to gain; projects which supply direct advantage to the public and projects which help the community, rather than specialist activity groups. The Foyle Foundation has been especially good at funding library and ICT developments in schools.

- *Example*: a school received a £5,000 grant to have its library upgraded, including a special section on environmental issues.

★ *Frederick Soddy Trust*

www.soddy.org

Grants of up to £850 are available for fieldwork projects, with those projects including a strong element of human geography being favoured. A report must be provided to the trust on completion. Application is made via a 500-word statement which must be returned by the deadline of 15 December.

- *Example*: the Settle Millennium Map project was funded through this trust (see page 108).

★ *Global School Partnerships starter grants*

www.camb-ed.com/home/Aboutus/NotforprofitFoundation/DGSPStarterGrant/tabid/1354/Default.aspx

This is an ideal funding scheme for schools embarking on a collaborative project with a school overseas in order to promote global learning through the curriculum. Grants of £250 are provided through the Department for International Development to support schools in finding a partner to work with. The funds are intended to fund supply cover and travel to workshops on the Global School Partnerships scheme, or in-school training by a Development Education Centre.

★ *Human Scale Education*

www.hse.org.uk

Provides grants for education projects with a strong human dimension. Human Scale Education is an education reform movement committed to small-scale learning communities based on the values of democracy, fairness and respect, in which children and young people are known and valued as individuals. Applications can be submitted any time.

- *Example*: the Settle Environment Fair project was funded through this trust (see page XX).

★ *Learning through Landscapes*

www.ltl.org.uk

Joining this charity with give you access to expertise that can fast-track you to a range of funding opportunities to make your school grounds a better resource for learning. Applications can be submitted any time.

- *Example*: a school received grants up to the value of £10,000 to help transform its grounds into a superb learning zone. The grants enabled the creation of a sensory garden, a pond and a sculpture trail.

★ *Ray Y Gildea Jr. award*

www.rgs.org/OurWork/Grants/Teaching/Ray+Y+Gildea+Jr+Award.htm

This scheme, administered by the Royal Geographical Society, supports innovation in geography teaching and learning in secondary and higher education. The outcomes of the grant should show direct benefits to students in geography. A single grant of £1,000 is awarded annually, with the deadline for applications falling in mid October.

- *Example*: the 2009 award winner was 'A virtual journey across Greenland', a project which aims to inspire and create a sense of curiosity in geography students by demonstrating live science while crossing the Greenland icecap with dog teams. It aims to make polar science more accessible and real in the classroom through the use of virtual technologies.

★ *Royal Geographical Society innovative teaching grants*

www.rgs.org/OurWork/Grants/Teaching/Innovative+Geography+Teaching+Grants.htm

This excellent scheme aims to fund innovative geography teaching in secondary schools. The grants are designed to enable geography teachers to develop imaginative or creative teaching materials and teaching methods. The aim is to serve both geography students and the wider teaching community. Each year, five grants of £800 are offered, and the deadline for applications falls in mid October.

- *Example*: previous grants have gone to a wide range of projects, including an online international weather station, a geography and the internet project and the creation of a multifaceted geography courtyard.

★ *Royal Meteorological Society*

www.rmets.org

For £15, schools can join the society which gives them access to grants to purchase meteorological equipment, carry out fieldwork and encourage the study of meteorology in schools. Grants can also be obtained for professional development.

★ *Royal Society science partnership grants*

http://royalsociety.org/partnership

Although this scheme is aimed mainly at science teachers, there are opportunities for geography teachers wishing to explore the scientific side of the subject. Funding of £3,000 is available to support teachers, scientists and engineers working together to inspire young people. The aim is to enrich teaching by bringing scientific study alive in schools. All projects must involve a teacher and a practising scientist/engineer who is external to the school. The deadline for applications falls in November.

- *Example*: a school received a grant of £2,200 to fund a project to investigate the effects of water quality on the biodiversity of the river Thames.

★ *SIFA educational trust*

www.plans-ltd.co.uk/trusts/index.htm

This is a funding body dedicated to channelling resources into schools. As well as bursary schemes to partly cover fees for certain students, there are grants available to fund educational projects, books, equipment and school trips. Bids must be submitted by 31 January, and there is no minimum or maximum grant amount.

★ *Trees for Schools fund*

www.treecouncil.org.uk

This is a funding scheme that will help you plant trees on your school grounds, which can then be used as a learning resource in geography (and other) lessons. Schools are able to apply for trees for projects up to £700 in value, with 75 per cent of the costs being provided by the Trees for Schools grant (the remainder will need to be raised by your school). Eligible costs include the trees themselves and any necessary supports and aids to establishment such as stakes and fertilizer. The spirit of the scheme is to involve students as closely as possible in the planting and maintenance of the trees.

★ *Volvo adventure competition*

www.volvoadventure.org/home.aspx

This award scheme, run by Volvo in partnership with the United National Environment Programme, is especially suitable for teachers wishing to develop geography enrichment projects with an environmental flavour. Cash awards of up to $10,000 are offered to groups of students who carry out an environmental project in their local community, plus the chance to win a trip to Gothenburg to take part in a young person's conference on the environment. The group must contain between two and five members between the ages of 13 and 16, and a report of the project must be submitted electronically. The deadline for submission falls in January.

- *Example*: a Russian school won the 2008 award scheme with a project that saved a local nature park from destruction by industry. The students cleaned up the park and gave it a new life so that the community could re-engage with it.

★ *Young Roots heritage lottery*

www.hlf.org.uk/HowToApply/programmes/Pages/youngroots.aspx

Young Roots is a grant programme designed to engage young people aged 13–25 with their heritage, with up to £25,000 being offered. The project should stem from the interests and ideas of young people who are supported by schools to develop skills, build confidence and connect with their local communities. A further aim is to make links between schools and heritage organizations, so you should consider which local organizations you could partner with. Applications can be submitted at any time.

- *Example*: a school received a grant of £9,000 to investigate the biodiversity of a series of wild flower meadows close to the school site, in partnership with a local natural history society. Students learned about the ecology and management of the site and developed their fieldwork skills.

Funds from income generation

The following is a list of funding sources which can help you generate cash for your school, which can then be spent on anything you want, to improve standards for students. Additionally, the box gives five innovative ideas for raising funds through events. A concerted effort to maximize funds from the sources listed below could bring your school over £5,000 in unrestricted funds.

★ *Bag 2 School*

www.bag2school.com

Bag 2 School is a business which pays £200 per tonne to schools for unwanted second-hand clothing. It offers an off-the-shelf solution for school fund-raising, helps the environment, and provides employment at home and abroad. The majority of the clothing is shipped to wholesalers in Latvia, Lithuania and Africa, where it is sold in its original state to the general public through retailers. Schools have been successful in raising over £1,000 through the Bag 2 School scheme.

★ *Ink cartridge recycling*

www.cashforcartridges.co.uk

There are substantial sums of money to be made by selling used printer cartridges to specialist dealers, who then refill them and sell them on to the public. Some schools have managed to raise over £500 a year by collecting such cartridges from the school printers and also making an appeal to parents and the wider community. A range of companies specialize in this sort of recycling, with the details of your local companies appearing in the yellow pages. A national company specializing in this type of recycling is Cash for Cartridges.

★ *Mobile phone recycling*

www.recycool.org

In common with used printer cartridges, unwanted mobile phones can similarly be sold to specialist dealers who harvest usable parts from them. Once again, a sum in the region of £500 is attainable if you manage to get everyone in the school community on-board. Again, the Yellow Pages should be your first port of call. A national company specializing in mobile phone (and printer cartridge) recycling is Recycool.

★ *Paper recycling*

Some schools manage to bring in over £1,500 each year by organizing the collection of waste paper. Your first port of call if you want to investigate this lucrative source of funding would be your local paper merchant. While setting up such a scheme is sure to be labour intensive – at least initially – schools have successfully gained the support of an enthusiastic band of volunteers who have taken the lead in coordinating the collection.

Innovative income generation ideas for geography departments

- Geography photo competition – the school community is invited to enter a geographical photo competition where they have to take an image of geographical interest. Entries cost £1, and a prize donated by a local camera shop is given to the winning entry.

- Sponsored orienteering event – with students taking part to develop their map reading skills.
- Geography quiz night – teams of parents and students come along to an evening of geography questions (pub style) with prizes donated by local companies. A raffle held at night raises additional funds.
- Guided geography walks – students (perhaps in year 11 and above) are trained in the local geography around the school and then lead guided geography walks for members of the public who make a donation to the department for attending the walk. The student is rewarded through the provision of stationery for school use, together with the knowledge that they are putting their geographical skills to good use.
- Geography fact file – the department offers to prepare fact files on countries and cities being visited by parents and other members of the public on holidays. The students are responsible for preparing the fact files as part of their geography studies, and the recipients make a donation to the department upon receiving the fact file.

Task 5.1: Staying at the cutting edge

The books, magazines, websites, ICT tools, hands-on tools, organizations and funding sources listed above are all designed to help you keep your geography teaching at the cutting edge. Identify ten elements listed which are new to you, and consider how you will use them to improve your geography teaching. Time will inevitably be needed to research things further and plan; so, create a timeline for the next few weeks showing how you will divide up your time as you work to introduce the new ideas into your classroom. When you are in need of further inspiration, you can return to this list and choose another five things which you would like to work on.

Index

Page numbers in **bold** denote figures.